SUCCESS *Unwrapped*

Direct Sellers'
A–Z Events Guide

SUCCESS
Unwrapped

Direct Sellers'
A–Z Events Guide

* Stellar Sales
*Committed Customers
*Teams that Thrive

Shannon Ferraby

Published by DPWN Publishing
A division of the Dynamic Professional Women's Network, Inc.
1879 N. Neltnor Blvd. #316, West Chicago, IL 60185
www.overcomingmediocrity.org
www.ourdpwn.com

Printed in the United States of America

Teagan Ferraby/Illustrator

ISBN: 978-1-939794-13-0

Forward

"If someone would have told me back in 1992 that I, by myself, would end up crisscrossing America selling my wares at craft shows, fairs, and boutiques to the tune of hundreds of thousands of dollars each year, I just wouldn't have believed them.

Or that I would assemble a team of like-minded sellers who would join me to do the same to the tune of millions of dollars' worth of merchandise at similar events across the country. I would have asked them to put down their beer, pick up a cup of coffee, and wake the heck up.

That was never was on my radar, ever.

And yet, that is what I have done and continue to do.

There wasn't a Shannon Ferraby of *Success Unwrapped* fame guiding me with amazing tips on how to not only sell products but how to build a customer base and suggest to me I follow up and show I care. When you read the book, Shannon will guide you on how to successfully perform these and other essential concepts.

To think that at one point I just ignored thousands of potential customers pains me. What a missed opportunity. Did I find a measure of success despite my woeful lack of follow up? Yes, I did, but holy moly, imagine what kind of organization I could have amassed much quicker with her well thought out, tested suggestions on how to maximize the gifts direct selling events create in the quest to build a successful network marketing business. And for any of you wondering just how legit her suggestions are, I recently worked a large, successful event with Shannon, and I will tell you flat out – SHE PRACTISES WHAT SHE PREACHES! Every one of her tips were on display and succeeding. Take it from a guy who has done hundreds of events. This is the missing handbook for craft shows, fairs, and events that will guide you to success!"

John Dorsey

CEO, Lilla Rose Inc

Dedication

I'm thankful to God and pray that in all I do I honor Him.

For my parents, my husband, Marc, and our five children, thank you for encouraging me and your confidence in my ability to accomplish my dreams! It's not weird to you that I get these crazy ideas and run with them, it's just who I am. Thank you for loving me with all my craziness and business and my seemingly incapability to slow down—ever!

For my friend and assistant, Jessica. I couldn't have done this without you.

For my lovely Lilla Rose ladies, you let me be your leader when I had nothing to lead with. You allowed me to give the only thing I had; myself, and you accepted my gift with love. Thank you will never be enough.

Introduction

If I told you that I went shopping for books at a homeschool convention and instead wound up finding the product that would launch me into my dream career and our family into earning a six-figure income, would you believe me? I wouldn't believe me either. But it's true! When I joined the world of direct sales, I didn't know it at first, but I invested in a big, gorgeous gift for myself and my family. I have spent years unwrapping all the wonder in that present and continually find myself in awe of the beauty and brilliance of this industry. In *Success Unwrapped, Direct Sellers' A-Z Event Guide*, I'm unwrapping all my secrets to grow your business through vending at craft fairs and other events.

Many trainers and experts in the direct sales industry would, at best, ignore the topic of vendor events and, at worst, try to steer you away from them. Not me! I am the top ranked consultant in our company and my thriving business was built upon vendor events! You can find books, webinars, podcasts, training sessions, and more on how to coach a hostess and step by step guides on how to hold a party. There is no shortage of great trainings for how to grow your business utilizing social media platforms, click funnels, and so on. But how do you grow a thriving business being a vendor at craft shows? How do you maximize your investment of time and money to reach your goals and dreams being a re-seller at a vendor event? There were no resources available to answer these questions. Until now.

For years I have been answering direct sales consultants' questions on how to not only survive but thrive in this industry. The question I get most often is,

"Shannon, *how did you do that* selling at craft shows?" I've unwrapped it all for you! With this book, you will know everything I have learned and shared with the thousands of ladies on my team. It is their questions that will lead you away from doubting if trying to grow your business while vending is a good idea, or even a possibility, to believing that you too can have the career of your dreams and provide a fantastic income for your family. Follow the secrets unwrapped in these pages and you will succeed! How can I be so sure? Because this book was written *for you* with the help of people *just like you*! I'm answering the very questions you have been contemplating, asked by real consultants in our industry. In this book, I am providing the solutions to obstacles you want to overcome and problems you didn't realize you have. The gift of success in your sales industry is in front of you. It's beautifully wrapped and waiting for you to rip off the ribbons, tear into the paper, and get to the success inside! Let's unwrap it together!

Table of Contents

A is for...
Approachable, Attire, & Available

"Your attire is representing you and your brand."
—Carla New, Senior Director, Origami Owl

Approachable

"Why are people passing my booth and not stopping?" —Krissy S., FL

Before we unwrap that answer, I've got to say, "Good for you!" You noticed that something is off. You looked around and noticed there are shoppers, but they aren't shopping with you. Below are the top complaints shoppers have about vendors and their displays. To answer your question, start by evaluating each of these areas and make changes as needed. Then enjoy unwrapping the secrets to your success with every chapter and every implemented change throughout the rest of this book!

Shoppers do not like a booth if...

1. It's cluttered. If you have too much stuff and it's not clear what you sell, instead of being curious and heading on over, they will be confused and keep on walking.

2. The consultant is not interested in them, not friendly, not helpful, or basically ignores the shoppers.
3. The consultant is "in your face" pushy, loud, or in other ways rude.
4. There are no signs clearly showing what you sell and what it does.
5. They can't see how much things cost without having to ask you.
6. There is not enough product to enjoy looking at.
7. It's confusing and the themes don't visually match.
8. There is no "draw" or eye catcher that makes them stop in their tracks and take a second look.
9. There are no cards to take with your information.
10. There are no discounts or specials.
11. There are no freebies or gifts.

Your booth or table at a craft show should be visually appealing and approachable. Not too cluttered, and easy for everyone to see clearly what you sell. Go for not only "approachable" but also "touchable." According to the Direct Sales Association, 68% of Americans don't like shopping online because they can't see, touch or try on what they are buying. Shoppers enjoy booths where they are not afraid to pick things up and get a closer look!

Attire

"How should I dress for an event?" —Michele C., PA

Senior Director with Origami Owl, Carla New, puts it this way: "Your attire is representing you and your brand. Always present yourself as clean and neat. Dressing casual is okay, depending on the event, but be sure to have your clothes free of wrinkles. I try to wear clothes with my company's logo. If that is not possible, I will wear our colors."

In addition to Carla's excellent advice, I would add these additional considerations:

- Dress for success. Project the image you want to convey. You are a professional and you are successful. Casual, but professional casual or one step up can set a successful tone. Some attire choices are just a "no-no."

- o Don't wear a business suit to a 4-H outdoor fair.
- o Leave your daisy dukes and any other revealing clothing at home.
- o Heels are pretty, but your feet might disagree after 6-8 hours in those babies!
- o Any clothing that has stains, rips, or is dirty needs to visit the laundromat, not your event.

- In addition to your choice of clean, branded if possible, comfortable, casual but still nice, clothes and comfy shoes, your appearance involves more than just your outfit.
  - o Cleanliness is a virtue and a priority to your appearance—nails, hair, and teeth included.
  - o Hair styling and makeup are optional, based on your personal style and preference. I am not in agreement when consultants are told they must go all out and dress up, including tons of makeup, to be successful at sales. Unless, of course, you sell make up. Then by all means, you ought to be wearing it and representing what you sell. And if you sell hair accessories, you ought to be wearing and demonstrating those. Regardless of what you sell, your hair should be clean and neat and your makeup should be in good taste if you wear it.
  - o Smells matter. Since I've worked at hundreds of events, I know that it is an area that is either not considered or sometimes forgotten by some vendors. If I am shopping at a booth, and the person working that booth smells bad, I will not stay. Done deal. I'm outta there! I know I am not the only one. Shopping, especially a day out at a craft show, should be a pleasant experience. There is nothing pleasant about being in a small, confined booth space with someone who smells bad. That's why I always keep deodorant and breath mints in my craft show bags.

- Body language. Many consultants realize that what they wear and how they dress can affect how others view them and interact with them. There is another consideration that is very often overlooked. What are you "wearing" and communicating with your body language?

- o According to nonverbalgroup.com, various studies show that 60-90% of what we communicate to others happens through our body language, not our words. "Nonverbal behavior is the most crucial aspect of communication." Recognize that you communicate most when you express through four areas of body language: eyes, face, torso, and arms and legs.

- o First impressions matter, and you only get one first impression. The first impression you give to your shoppers may happen before they see or care about your attire and before you have a chance to say a word. When they are down the row, in the next aisle, or standing at another booth, and just happen to glance in your direction, what will your body language tell them?

- o Do you know the Golden Rule? Bob Burg of Endless Referrals says it is, "All things being equal, people will do business with, and refer business to, those people they know, like and trust." Consultants need to intentionally project body language that communicates that you are a likeable and trustworthy person they should get to know and do business with.

  - Standing and leaning in when someone is speaking projects a positive, "I'm interested" message.

  - Keep your arms and hands open, not crossed or closed, or they may think you are closed off.

  - Smile, with your mouth and with your eyes.

  - Standing at a slight angle, rather than straight on (just put one foot forward), is more comfortable and less "in their face"

  - Pay attention with your eyes, your body, and your mind to anyone talking to you and the people around you. Put away your phone, or they might assume from your body language that you are "too busy" or "not interested" in helping them.

- Keep your general posture confident and engaged. Don't tap your fingers, fidget or slump, giving the appearance that you are bored.

Available

"Should I offer to help everyone who comes near my table? Or let them browse and only step in if they ask for help?" —Kim F., OK

Be available but not "in your face." There is a difference. Customers should know that if they need help, you are happy to give it. No one enjoys being followed, pestered or hovered over when they are browsing. We talked about body language and what you are conveying with yours, but you should also observe the body language of your shoppers and learn how to step back from their space if you are crowding them. Offer to help and check in occasionally when they have been there for some time, but don't hover or come across as pushy.

I'll never forget when Shelly and Kirk, a lovely middle-aged couple, walked into my tent at my first outdoor event. She was drawn to the sparkle of the hair clips I was selling, and he was anxious to see something pretty in her blonde, curly hair. As we chatted, I twisted her hair up into a beautiful style in seconds. His eyes lit up. He started complimenting her immediately and wanted to be sure the curly tendrils that naturally hung out of the style and framed her face stayed just so. She left with the clip I put in her hair, both of them smiling. I was struck by how kind he was to her and imagined they were in a new relationship. Shelly emailed me later, and as we corresponded, I learned that Kirk was actually her husband of many years! Kirk and Shelly became huge supporters of my business, both through purchasing, hosting, and sharing with friends. A few years later at that same outdoor event, Shelly stopped in to say hi. We chatted, and she shared that someone whom she was trying to help had stolen many of the hair clips she bought from me. Kirk popped in later, but before he left, I gave him one of Shelly's favorite clips in her size. He was visibly touched, and Shelly returned shortly after to thank me, too. It was so easy to give to them, though. Their support helped me launch my business and their friendship had been a blessing to our entire family. I was delighted to have a small opportunity to say thanks. Business growth, friendship, and an opportunity to give back all came because I made myself available at one local show.

—Kristen Smith, Director, Lilla Rose

B is for...
Bags & Bookings

*"Your business is building your dreams for you, so
let those dreams be louder than your fears."*
—Tamara Allen, Founding Director, Magnolia and Vine

Bags

***"Wow! You check people out fast! What are in those bags you hand them,
anyway?" —Jean C., OH***

It's not enough to show up the day of the event and hope for the best. You should be planning and preparing before the show. Practice your display, collect your needed supplies, and label all marketing materials. Work hard after the show by following up with every shopper as well as anyone else who provided you with their contact information.

For speedy checkout, have your bags pre-stuffed before the show begins. I bring extra bags and items to stuff in them in case I underestimated the number I need.

Here are some ideas of what to put in your shopper bags:

- a business card
- a thank you note for their purchase
- warranty, guarantee, and exchange information
- any specials you are offering soon
- a list of upcoming shows you will be attending
- any instructions they might need to use your product
- how to join your VIP customer group on Facebook
- an invitation to post a photo using or wearing what they just purchased and tag your business page to be entered into a contest.
- how to find and follow you on your social media pages.

Every single piece of marketing material you place in the bag needs to be labeled with your website, phone number, email, and social media addresses. Consider that shoppers have different preferences for communicating. Perhaps you love texting and contemplated only putting your number to text as your contact information. Don't do it! Provide every means to contact you and allow shoppers to reach out in the way that best suits them. Don't put contact information on just your business card, for example, and assume since it is there the rest do not need it. They may only keep one item out of everything you put in the bag. If it's not the business card, they will not be able to contact you. Considering 88% of business cards are thrown away within the first week (see Customer Care for more info), that is even more reason to label everything; the business card alone will not suffice.

Bookings

"How do I book parties from shows?" —*April B., TX*

It is common for many consultants to sing the same song. It's called the "I've Got No Bookings Blues." Much of your success, in booking parties and all areas of this business, is going to depend more on *you* than your circumstances. How you respond to your circumstances, how much you are willing to work towards your goals, how you put your product out there, and how you respond to interest. I am going to give you some fabulous ideas, tips, and methods to book parties from your shows. However, if you do not put these ideas, or some of your own, into effect, you will forget all about them and be singing the "I've Got No Bookings Blues" all over again. To really get the most out of this section, I'm going to encourage you to be an active participant. So, go grab a pen.

Are you back? Ready? Awesome!

Now, make a list of all your excuses. Why don't you have the bookings for the parties you want to hold for your business?

_____
_____
_____
_____
_____

How many did you come up with? I had about eight when I first made my list. Everything from I don't know enough people, I'm afraid to ask, to I didn't plan, I didn't follow up well, and more.

Now, here comes the fun part! Pick that pen back up and cross off those excuses you just wrote down! Scribble away and black them out! Unless, of course, you don't really want to get more bookings. If you *would* really like to have bookings and learn how to get them from being a vendor at shows, then grab a Sharpie! Go to town and get rid of those excuses! Because that's all they are. They are not good reasons. They are a lame attempt at making ourselves feel justified for not doing what we say we really want to do. Excusing yourself is appropriate sometimes. Like when you sneeze or bump into someone. When you don't have the bookings you want and need to grow your business and reach your goals, that is no time for excusing any behavior or lack of it. That is the time for making changes and making progress! Not making excuses. Have I convinced you yet? Did you cross them all out? Are you ready to do this thing? Awesome!

Set work hours

You are a business owner. Whether you choose to work full time or part time is up to you. You set your own goals and you need to do the work and make the

9

effort to meet those set goals. Set aside a certain amount of time every day, not just the hours you are working at your craft or vendor events, for your business. Use that scheduled and structured time to accomplish the things you are going to read about in this section. While you are reading, if an idea pops into your head, jot it down in the margin. My hope is that these ideas will be the spark to light a fire under you to stop making excuses, to come up with more of your own creative and productive ideas, and get those parties booked!

Decide

Make a firm decision that you are willing to and are going to invest in yourself and the growth of your business. Many of the ideas shared in this book will take work and time, and some of them will take a financial investment as well. How much can you invest in your business? If that is not a question you have previously answered, now would be a good time to put some thought into it. Refer to chapter R to read more about risk and making wise decisions for your business.

Put it to paper

After you read through this chapter and are excited about the ideas, develop a plan and write it down. Tell your spouse, or your sponsor in your company, or choose someone to tell what your intentions are. Choose someone you know will be your cheerleader, never someone who will vocalize doubt in your ideas or ability. Hang your list of steps to reach your goals somewhere you will see them often. The more you talk about and see your action steps, the more likely you will be to follow through with them.

Do something different

What approaches have you taken in the past to try to book parties while at your vendor events, or after the fact with the people you met? Do you normally email them? Do you typically ask them in person at the show? Have you been collecting their phone numbers and calling and leaving messages? Do you send them on their way with a flyer in their bag inviting them to be a hostess? If you have never tried to book parties from a show, then you can plough full steam ahead with any of the options I am going to share. They are all "doing something different" in your situation, and good for you for making changes and progress!

If you have, however, been putting forth effort and trying to book parties with little to no positive results, it's time to mix it up or step it up! To continue to do the same things, over and over, that are not working for you? Well, that would drive anyone crazy! As Einstein said, "The definition of insanity is doing the same thing over and over again but expecting different results."

Make a list

Create a list of potential hostesses using contacts from previous events you have already worked and more. There is no need to recreate the wheel. Moving forward, yes, you are going to try some new and exciting things when you get to your next vendor event. But why wait until then? Many of you have worked events in the past and you have contacts from those events and other areas in your life that are great leads for future hostesses.

Create a list including:

- Anyone who said they might host in the future
- Anyone who has hosted a party with you in the past
- Guests from any parties you have held in the past
- Anyone who keeps popping into your mind
- Customers who have purchased from you at events or online
- Show organizers you have been building a relationship with

Start jotting names down here if a piece of paper isn't handy, but later, move them to a place where you will continue to grow the list and can keep track as you make connections.

_____

_____

_____

_____

_____

What's the matter? Were you not able to fill up those lines above and are now feeling sorry for yourself, thinking something like, "See? I just don't have a good list! I can't even fill up five silly little lines and don't even need to move to a regular piece of paper!" I caught you! Where did you put that Sharpie?

If I am right, and you were thinking something along those lines, then you are just back to singing those booking blues. Remember, you are reading this book for a great reason! You want to work at craft shows and other vendor events and you want to unwrap their full potential to help you succeed in your business and reach your goals! If you already had a booming, six-figure or more direct selling business, with customers knocking down your door to buy from you, host parties, and join your team, you likely would not be reading this book. You are reading in the awesome company of many direct selling consultants around the world, who, like you, are ready to take this incredible opportunity and unwrap its full potential! It's expected that you don't already have everything in place and lists of contacts out the wazoo! Just start with what you have and remember, you don't have to have everything in place to get started, but you do have to get started to eventually have everything in place. In addition to that truth, you only need one person to say yes to hosting an in-home event to get yourself off and partying! Even before your next event you can work on getting one yes from whatever contacts you currently have. When your next event comes, try some of the ideas in this chapter for creative ways to get even more yeses!

Seasonal specials

During winter months, for example, offer a "hot," can't pass it up deal to winter hostesses. Tell them your deal is so hot, it is sure to take away their winter chill.

Double credit

Whatever your company offers for hostess rewards, offer to personally double it for a limited amount of time for parties that qualify by reaching a certain amount of sales.

Free mystery gift

Offer a free mystery gift valued at a specified amount for hostesses who book their party with you that day at the craft show. Their gift is given to them when the party is held.

Basket of all baskets

Decide on a theme for your basket and then go all out! It should be so amazing, so incredible, that if someone asked you to host a party, and you knew you might win that basket for doing it, *you* would say yes!

A few fun ideas include:

- A romance basket: wine, candle, chocolate, etc.

- Beat the winter blues basket: family games, fun movies, popcorn, etc.

- Warming you up: hot chocolate, cozy socks, soft blanket, gloves, candle, etc.

- Splashing summer fun: beach bag, beach towel, sun glasses, tickets to a local water park, etc.

- Falling in love: fall-colored décor items, candle, a good book, cozy scarf, etc.

- Spring to life: brightly colored spring scarf, spring scented candle, flower seed packets, etc.

What other creative ideas popped into your mind? Jot them down here so you don't forget your brilliance!

_____

_____

_____

_____

To really make this basket idea work, you truly need to go all out! Make it stunning! Jaw dropping! The kind of basket that stops people in their tracks to see what is in it and then they think, *I want it!* Take this amazing basket with you to shows and any parties you already have booked, and take a photo of it everywhere else you go. You never know when you might wind up having a conversation with someone about booking a party. And you can't exactly carry this basket with you, as gorgeous as it is, to go grocery shopping!

Show off the basket and excitedly explain that every hostess who books and holds her party by such and such a date earns an entry to win this basket. Add that you only have six openings! That means this amazing basket prize is going to be a 1 in 6 chance for a hostess to win! The value of the basket, if done well, could be as high as about $100! This is an investment in your business. But let's do a little simple math. Zero parties booked right now = spending zero but also earning zero. Spend $100 on this basket, then book and hold 6 parties, where you will earn an average of $200-$400 per party (based on your company's party average). That alone could equal $1200-$2400 in profit! That's not even counting all the business you will get and growth you will see when you follow my tips in the section on follow up! Wow! That $100 basket is looking like a pretty worthwhile investment right now, isn't it?

Open date cards

You never know when you might be chatting with someone and the subject of hosting a party will come up. Certainly, when working at your show, you should be intentional about it coming up. When someone expresses interest, have an open date card ready to pull out and fill in! Each open date card should have two weeks of dates on the front and two weeks on the back. Work on filling the first side before turning it over to the back. Fill in any spaces that you are not available with "full." Write "open" on the dates you have open for parties and point to those. Say, "These are the dates I have open over the next few weeks, which works best for you?" You will be helping your hostess by narrowing down her choices for her. Once she selects a date from your open date card, simply fill her basic information into that space and promise to get in touch with her right away after the event. Be sure she has your information and any information you hand out about hosting a party as well. Now that her selected date is in writing, she will feel more committed and be less likely to cancel. Of course, be willing to be flexible. When you get in touch with her the next day, if she got home and realized that date had a conflict, you simply pull your open date card back out and offer her the next few choices you have available.

Book Bonus:

Your Free Open Date Card: www.bit.ly/SuccessUnwrappedBookBonus

Book to Pop

Pick up an inexpensive helium tank at a party store or Wal-Mart. Grab a bag of latex balloons and some ribbon. The morning of your show, fill out little slips of paper with prizes written on them. Make most valued at $5-$15 but one at about a $50 value. Before blowing up the balloons, put the prize slips inside.

Once the balloons are blown up, write on them with a Sharpie. In big letters, write "BOOK TO POP!" On one write "$5?" and on other balloons write "$15?" "$50!?!" $10?" The balloons, all by themselves, will attract attention and people will ask what they are. If they don't, you simply say, "Who is ready to book to pop?" And shoppers will ask, "Book what? What do I get?" Explain that the first five (or however many balloons you have) ladies to book their home party with you that day will get the extra bonus of choosing and popping a balloon! Inside each one is an extra gift they will receive on top of the already generous hostess rewards! Curiosity is a fun and powerful tool, and ladies who were on the fence will jump right on the side of yes to have a chance at not only popping a balloon to satisfy their curiosity of what is inside, but also for the chance to win an extra gift! When someone is ready to pop, take out your open date card and get their date and information down before you let them pop.

Ask her if it's okay for you to video or take her photo for your VIP page while she pops! It's a great opportunity for you to share how exciting it is to be one of your hostesses! The one booking and popping will want to be added to your VIP group to see herself in the video or photo. There are many similar approaches to Book to Pop, such as: envelopes with varying prizes listed inside, pretty gift bags with the actual prize inside, and wrapped little boxes. My favorite at craft shows is the Book to Pop because it is dramatic, fun, and attracts a lot of extra attention to your booth.

No matter which of these incentives to book you try, remember:

- Make it attractive. You are marketing to women. What the envelopes, balloons, or gift bags look like will have an impact on their desire to open them enough to book a party in that moment. Think pretty colors, raffia, tissue paper, ribbons. Make sure they complement your display and branding.
- The hostess does not actually get the extra gift until the night of her party.

Booking from bookings

Once you have your first yes, a party booked, you want to try to get at least one, but hopefully two to three, bookings from that party. Display a poster that you made with the hostess benefits, deck the hostess out with a sample of what hostesses earn, play some type of booking game, and use some of the same approaches shared above for your events at the home party. There are plenty of trainings and resources available for how to have a successful in-home party, so I'm not going into those details. However, I will mention that you have your snowball rolling with your first yes! The last thing you want is to steamroll it flat by not putting in the work and effort to make the party the best it can be for you, your hostess, and her guests! Go all out and make it so much fun that they would be crazy *not* to say yes when you invite them to host their own! No one wants to go to someone else's house and sit and listen to speeches or feel pressured to buy. Don't do that to your hostess and her friends. Make it the best night of their month!

Here are just a few ideas of some fun themes you can incorporate (and advertise about at your shows):

- **Cash for clunkers party!** They bring their old, worn-out items that your product line can replace. You give a small discount ($1 off, for example) for them trading in their old for your new. In my company, we sell hair accessories. It is always so much fun to encourage guests to bring their oldest, ugliest hair clip or other accessory. You could even do a contest for the worst one, and they get double the discount!

- **Nutty Buddy party!** It's a home party with a twist and a split! A banana split, that is! Hostesses team up with a friend and each invite guests. Everyone parties together, makes banana splits for a delicious treat, and the buddy hostesses split the rewards! This would be a great theme for when you are willing to offer double hostess rewards. They get to enjoy all the fun together and both earn the generous rewards in full. Double the hostesses, double the rewards, double the guests, and double the fun!

- **Painting party**! Have a fun sign advertising it at your craft show and allow ladies to sign up to join you. They pay to paint, bring their friends for a great night out, and shop your products! Have special prizes and giveaways to make the night even more exciting! Perhaps one of the guests will win her painting fee as a prize!

- **Happy un-birthday Mommy & Me party!** This is a fun option for a hostess who is a stay at home Mom and prefers an event during the day.

Moms can bring their kids, so babysitting is not a worry. Suggest the hostess lightly decorate like a kid's birthday party and serve cupcakes and ice cream. Everyone will love the fun atmosphere. Moms can shop while kids play! Keep in mind, you will not be able to cover your demonstration and information in the same way that you do at an evening event with no children. But these awesome moms deserve the chance to get together and hear all about your fabulous products and opportunities. Advertising at your show and bringing it up as an option will mean a lot to these busy moms of littles who sometimes feel left out from all the ladies' night fun!

I think I hear you singing a new song now! No more excuses, no more "I've Got No Bookings Blues"! You are singing the song of success because we've just unwrapped so much to be excited about! Jot down below your party action plan. Which idea jumped out at you the most? I suggest writing that one down and trying it first.

_____

_____

_____

You now have a lot of creative and wonderful ideas to get booking!

In a survey of over 360 consultants in direct sales, when questioned about how often, if at all, they ask shoppers at events about hosting a party, only 1.5% of them replied that they verbally ask *each* person who shops with them. While 25% "sometimes" ask some shoppers, 19% have a sign on their table advertising the hostess opportunity, and 25% put information about hosting in the shopper's bags. 15% don't bring it up during events, but will if they follow up and 14.5% do not ask customers about hosting a party.

I want to end this chapter with the best and most important idea of them all. The very best, and easiest way to get parties booked.

Just ask.

C is for...
Cash & Carry & Customer Care

"A sale is a dead end. If you don't create a system for follow up and continued communication, you're wasting your time."
—*Melissa Fietsam, Senior Executive Director, Thirty-One Gifts*

Cash & Carry

"Should you invest in and bring inventory to a craft show?" —***Amy W., OK***

The short answer is yes. Whenever possible, bring at least some cash and carry items with you. Most customers at a craft show prefer to purchase what they fall in love with, want or need, that day. Of course, they can't and won't buy everything they like and see. If you have cash and carry available, they will be more likely to choose your items over someone else's who is only accepting orders. A word of caution: vendor events are often a financial risk. You need to pay for the space and other expenses. Forking out more money for inventory increases your risk factor of losing instead of gaining from the event. There are fabulous opportunities at these events for you to share your business, expose others to you, your personal brand, your company and products, book home parties, make connections with fellow vendors, obtain helpful information about future events, build your business team, and more! Please don't be discouraged if you make a wise business decision to *not* invest in inventory at this time.

"How do you hold a successful craft show or vendor sale with a limited amount of cash and carry stock?" —*Allie B., MN*

Success is in the eyes of the cash and carry beholder. Success is also in the eyes of the one not beholding cash and carry. Without any, or a limited amount of cash and carry, your success is due to a different focus and measured with a different stick. Every event has much more potential than just cash in your pockets from re-selling the inventory you have purchased. In fact, that is one reason many team leaders discourage their consultants from working their business through vendor events. The temptation to put too much focus on the sales and miss the other equally, if not more, important business aspects is strong! Yes, it's wonderful to go home with that fast, earned cash but it's even better to have weeks' worth of bookings to keep your business moving and new consultants joining and strengthening your team. As a vendor with little to no inventory to sell, your focus will weigh much heavier on booking and team building. Consider this event a fabulous opportunity to share your business, you, your brand, and all you have to offer. Book home parties, share the business opportunity, and go home with a smile knowing you just unwrapped incredible potential growth for your business.

"Can you be successful at a vendor event without inventory and take orders or sell online at the event?" —*Jennifer R., IA*

You can be very successful, but not if you define success as getting a lot of shoppers to place orders that day or soon after. Most shoppers at events are spontaneous, purchasing items as they see them and fall in love with them. If a vendor doesn't have what they want available to purchase that day, they may say "Oh, okay, I'll just place an order when I get home." But be aware, most do not. This is a great opportunity for you to get their contact information and follow up to help them place that order, because odds are against them placing it otherwise. Certainly, bring a device to take their orders, or suggest they pull up your website on their phone and give placing orders a try. But you will leave feeling more successful if your goals are geared towards sharing your business, booking parties, providing information, and planting seeds about the business opportunity.

"How do you determine how much inventory to carry?" —April B., TX

My short answer is don't buy more than you can afford to take home with you after the event. If you have money to invest and know that if the products don't sell at one show, you have other events lined up soon after, then invest in enough to fill your display with backups to restock as items sell. The worst-case scenario is that you sell out! That is a very exciting problem to have. If that happens, you will know for next time to invest in more inventory for that event.

"Can you have too much inventory?" —Rhashell R., IN

Yes.

- You have too much inventory if it doesn't sell and when you leave you are in a financial hardship, unable to pay an upcoming bill or other needed expense that you hoped to cover with the sales of said inventory.

- You have too much inventory if you bought enough to last a long time but only have one event booked. It would be wise to start with what you think you need at your first event and build up your inventory over time as you start earning.

- You have too much inventory if it has an expiration date and doesn't sell in a timely manner and must be thrown away.

- You have too much inventory on your display (but maybe not too much in general) if your table is a cluttered mess and people can barely tell what it is that you sell. There is no need to put out everything you brought with you. Replace items as you sell the sample on display and mix up the variety of what you are showing throughout the day.

Customer Care

"How do you turn a one-time customer at a craft show into a repeat customer?"—Brittany B., OH

There is a big difference between a shopper and a customer. To build a strong and successful business, you need a steady increase of the latter. A shopper is someone who has money to spend and is on a mission to do it! They may have a specific purchase or gift recipient in mind, or they might not. In the case of a shopper walking into a craft show, they are most likely planning to shop but don't always know ahead of time for what or with whom. Who they choose to shop with and give their money to will be based on many contributing factors you are unwrapping in this book. If they choose to shop with you, which, of course, I hope they do, the first time they buy, they are still a shopper. They are not *your* customer. You happen to be one of the vendors they shopped with that day. You will find plenty of shoppers at craft shows. It will be up to you to develop those first-time shopping interactions into long-term customer relationships.

A customer is a shopper who is choosing to buy from a particular person or brand. Constant review of how to best meet shoppers' needs, evaluating how well they are satisfied on a regular basis, and developing a relationship with them beyond the sale is how you will turn a one-time shopper into your customer. In simpler terms, you need to provide outstanding customer care.

Shoppers turn into customers and will purchase products from consultants:

- They at first feel comfortable with and then grow to know, like, and trust
- Who treat them well
- Who contact them on a regular, but not annoying, basis
- Who they develop a personal connection with

There are three important points of contact you should focus on that show shoppers, soon to be your customers, you care.

1. First Impressions

Whether you first meet someone at a craft show, a home party, or casually out and about living life, the first impression is the only first one you will get. Ask yourself, "What do I want them to see and remember about me?" As an entrepreneur who owns and manages your own business in the sales industry, you are never truly "off duty." Every interaction, with any person, could result in having just found your next amazing customer or rock star team member. Continually and consciously project your best self and what you want others to see as their first impression of you.

When people meet you, it should be impressed upon them that:

- You use and love the products you sell
- You are passionate about being a consultant and purposefully positive
- You are interested in them as a person and you are genuinely a fun and caring person
- You are a professional and you are successful in your business

2. Parting Company

According to a survey conducted by Statistics Brain Research Institute, 88% of business cards handed out will be thrown away in less than a week. That equates to about 9 out of every 10 cards you distribute being rubbish rather than creating relationships or repeat sales! Yes, giving your contact information is important, but you obviously cannot count on the shopper to keep your information and come back to you again and again. They will, or at least 88% of them will, throw away your information. They then have no way to contact you even if they want to, and therefore no thought of you or shopping with you should they even be interested in more of the products you sell.

Before your shoppers leave your booth or table, exchange contact information. When you really care about keeping in touch with someone, you don't just give them your information, you make sure that you have theirs. The impetus is on you, the person building the business and these relationships, to be in control. Guarantee that you can still connect with the 88% of shoppers who threw away your card.

Ensure you have their information by using:

- A receipt with every transaction. I suggest carbon copy receipt forms, that are not in a booklet, but can be individually placed on clip boards. The portion you keep provides you with their information.
- A wish list card. Create index-sized wish list cards. As the guests are browsing, encourage them to keep track of items they love on a wish list card. Before they leave, have them complete their contact information on the back and promise them you will let them know when any of their wish list items go on sale, or similar items become available that they might be interested in.

- A customer loyalty card. Create a punch card (on paper or using a punch card app). They get one punch for every item purchased, and upon reaching a certain number of purchases, they receive a special gift. Loyalty cards give your shoppers a reason to not throw away your card. With just a few more items, they will earn something free! That is a great reason to tuck the card away where they will not lose it. If you are using an actual card, as opposed to an app, be sure to consider it your business card and include all your contact information on it. When offering a loyalty program, you will need a list, index card file, or app on your phone to keep track of which shoppers have joined and to stay in touch with them. Remember, this is a contact exchange and provides *you* with *their* information.

- An entry for your prize drawing. It's easy to get lost in the moment at a craft show and think that success or failure lies in only one thing: selling the product. There are so many avenues towards success and it helps to step back and see this bigger picture. Even if you sell nothing all day, but have a giveaway, and therefore guests' contact information, you have succeeded! You now have a fresh list of people you can reach out to. Every person has the potential of not being just one new relationship or one new customer, but 250! "Each of us has a personal sphere of influence of about 250 people," says Bob Burg of Endless Referrals. Following the tips in this section, and providing excellent customer care, will ensure your new contact loves working with you, buying from you, and they will often be happy to recommend you to their friends.

  o When considering what to give away, ask yourself, "Would I be excited to win this? Would I give my contact information for a chance at it?" If the answer is no, then you might want to consider increasing the desirability of the prize.

  o Clearly communicate in writing, where the guests can see, what the purpose of them providing you with their contact information is. Will you be sending them monthly emails? A bi-monthly newsletter? It is not legal (or nice) to collect their information in the name of winning a prize only, and then solicit them for sales. That is not a way to gain their trust or to hope they will grow to like you. Upfront and honest is the best approach. According to Statista.com, 80% of consumers break up with a brand when companies use consumer data without consent.

o To add excitement to your giveaway, display a sign designating the various times you will be drawing winners throughout the day. If you can, select a winner every hour. To make the most of this approach, you need to gather a crowd around your booth before every drawing. You announce that it's almost time to draw the next name, allowing those last-minute people passing by to quickly get their name in the hat! Once you have a little (or big!) crowd, use that opportunity to demonstrate your product line. If your product can be demonstrated on other people, ask for models from the crowd to help show everyone how your items work. Don't make this a long demonstration. You have worked hard to draw a crowd and don't want them to walk away because they are bored or tired of waiting. Demo something quickly, with excitement, then get right to selecting the winner. After you announce the winner, you have gained the crowd's attention and have new potential shoppers to start the top of this hour. Collect additional names and keep them excited for the next drawing, only one hour away.

o Check with the show promoter to be certain that individual vendors are permitted to have their own giveaway at their booth.

Ensure they leave with your information by providing:

- A catalog
- Business card
- Thank you note in bag with purchase
- Punch card
- Receipt
- Prepared hostess packet for anyone that booked a party
- Flyers or brochures about your business opportunity or hosting a party

- Flyer listing your upcoming show dates and locations
- Pens, keychains, or other advertising merchandise

Remember to label everything you will be handing out to customers. I suggest printing out your labels far in advance of when you will need them. Enjoy a good movie one night while you label everything! Purchase peel and stick address labels and print them out with your name, website, email address, phone number, and social media info. It's important to include every option of contacting you because you never know which mode of communication your new connections will prefer.

3. Follow up

Follow up on what you have said you will do. Did you promise to send them information about hosting or joining? Then do it! Did you tell them you would reach out to them when there are sales or specials? Get on that! When asked why you need their contact information, did you respond that you would like to contact them and make sure they are satisfied with their purchases? Then by all means, reach out and ask them if they are. No one wants to shop with or continue to work with a person who is not reliable. You are a business owner, and part time or full time, we all have responsibilities to uphold. The success of your business, and more importantly your reputation, is at stake when your promises are not kept. Follow up.

"Ring! Ring!" Is that your phone? Huh, should you answer it? It doesn't look like a number you are familiar with. Wait a minute! You just did a craft show and passed out your contact information to thirty-five people! Answer it! Answer it politely. Recognize that you own a business and your phone is not just a device for aimlessly scrolling on Facebook but a tool to help you connect, build relationships, and reach your goals. When a customer calls and leaves a voice message or texts you, do your best to get back to them as promptly as possible. If a shopper saw you over the weekend, saved your card, and made the effort to call you with a question or has decided to purchase, host, or join, the last thing you want is to leave them hanging. According to Statista.com, 71% of consumers break up with brands because of unresponsive customer service.

It's too easy to find another consultant. That is exactly what they will do if they are interested or need help and you don't promptly respond to meet their needs. Don't let that happen to you.

Answer your phone, reply to your texts and emails, and return their calls. You put forth a good effort to print stickers, plaster them all over everything, and intentionally ensure every shopper left with your information. Don't waste that! Be receptive and excited when they contact you.

Make it a priority to follow up with your new contacts and repeat customers on a regular basis throughout the year. Here are some ideas on how to contact them. Get creative and come up with more ways and opportunities to keep in touch with your customers.

- Newsletter campaigns to update them on specials, sales, and new products.

- Mail new catalogs when they are released and inserts for current catalogs when they become available. Be sure to include a hand-written note for a personal touch.

- Call or text them about two days, two weeks and two months after they make a purchase to inquire about their satisfaction.

- Offer to help them with gift needs. This is especially fun around any holiday. Consider offering gift wrapping, including gift notes, and the possibility of shipping gifts to the recipients on their behalf. They don't need to take you up on every service you offer, but every service you offer takes you up one notch in their minds.

- Send reminders about the items on their wish list cards.

- Send occasional postcards to keep in touch, and consider offering a VIP customer special on occasion.

- Start a customer birthday club. Prior to their birthday, send them a certificate for a free item or a discount.

- Be sure you are offering the business opportunity and the exciting offer for them to earn rewards by hosting an event!

Don't forget to show your customers that you CARE

C: Courteous and caring

A: Attentive, available, and always appreciative

R: Relatable and reliable

E: Excited, easy to work with, and eager to help

With customer CARE like that, they won't want to shop with anyone else! If you don't make it a top priority to build a relationship with your shoppers and grow them into customers, they will have no loyalty to you and no one else but you will be to blame when they wind up shopping with someone else.

"How do I grow a customer base?" —Courtney M., IL

1. Start somewhere. Get out there with your products and services and use the tips found in this book to unwrap the benefits and help meet shoppers needs.
2. Ask for the sale. Don't be afraid after sharing to ask, "Would you like me to ring that up for you?" "Are you ready for me to total up your purchases?" "Should I put those in a bag for you?" "Will you be purchasing with cash or credit today?"
3. Be patient. Some seeds take a while to grow. The sales will come. As Carly Reeves, Black Status Level 2 Younique Presenter, says, "Don't focus on results. They will come. Consistent daily action is what will build your empire."
4. Give and get. Give your contact information and get theirs.
5. Follow up and build relationships. When they are ready to make a purchase, you will be the one that comes to mind.

"What if I'm not a 'people person'? How should I connect with customers?" —Grace S., NY

I have good news and bad news.

The bad news is that you are in the sales industry and by its very nature it is relational. Relational means "concerning the way in which two or more people or things are connected." To work and grow this business, especially at vendor events sometimes packed with people, you will have to accept and embrace that you are going to have to learn to be a people person.

- You do not need to be an extrovert.

- You do not need to be talkative.

- You do not need to talk fast or loudly.

- You *do* need to be interested in, care about, and be willing to invest in, help, and serve people. That's a people person. Maybe you are one after all and you just hadn't realized.

The good news is that even if you read the bad news and confirmed you are not a people person, you can develop into one. It is not a trait you must be born with. At each event, push yourself a little bit more to ask people questions and listen to their answers. You may be surprised at how quickly you determine that people are wonderful, fascinating, a pleasure to serve and make smile. Before you know it, you'll be bragging about what a "people person" you are.

"How do you manage the logistics of demonstrating, helping customers choose, and checking someone out all on your own?" —Kristi B., SC

- Preparation
    - Place order forms and attach pens to clipboards ready to hand to shoppers.
    - Pre-stuff check-out bags with everything shoppers need.
    - Think, plan, and practice what you will say and do when you get busy.
- Organization
    - Stand in front or to the side of your table. Ensure everything you need to checkout is within easy reach or on your person in apron pockets.
- Communication
    - Greet people who approach your booth, even while working with another shopper. Greet them with your eyes, a smile, and a hello they can hear.

- o Be honest. If you are in the middle of helping someone, let them know that you are just finishing up and will be right with them.
- o Ask permission. Kindly ask if they would mind if you finished checking your current person out and explain that you will be right with them.
- o Continue to talk to the crowd while personally helping an individual.
- Be courteous
  - o Consider your crowd. Do not spend tons of time on one person when others are waiting. It's okay to answer one question, then help another shopper. Check out one person and then offer to assist another. You don't need to stick by their side from the moment they approach until they walk away. Shoppers don't like Velcro vendors.

D is for...
Display & Disappointment

"We are all unique with different personalities and strengths. One huge key to succeeding, loving what you do, and avoiding burn-out, is to focus on your strengths, and not try to be someone you are not."
—*Paula Ramm, Jr. Executive Director, Lilla Rose*

Display

"How can you gain attention to your booth or table from across the room?"
— Brenda R., NH

- Bed risers are a great option for helping your table stand out, assuming your event is not specifically geared towards children shoppers. A table a bit higher than others will stand out from the crowd and provide a more comfortable shopping experience.

- Customers tend to look from left to right, keep that in mind while setting up. Your display will be more appealing if it flows easily on the eyes from left to right.

- Create varying heights to your display. Have some items on shelves, boxes, or racks, and others on the table.

- Consider large, visually appealing signs, balloons, or other items that will attract attention in a positive way without blocking any neighboring vendors.

- Stand back and look at your display from every angle your customers will view it. What do you think? Would you be attracted to get a closer look? How about from down the aisle? Or the next aisle over? What can you change or add or take away to make it more appealing?

"How do you find balance between clutter and tastefully decorated booths?"
—Rhashell R., IN

- You don't need huge, heavy, hard to transport and set up displays.
- Keep it simple.
- Brand to your company's colors and overall look.
- Don't add a lot of extras.
- Head to chapter "L" for "Less is More" You'll unwrap more fabulous tips on keeping your display looking great and clutter free!

"How do you make sure you get everything displayed without your table looking cluttered, especially when you have to work in a small space?"
—Crystall C., FL

- You would be better off *not* displaying everything, smooshing it all on the table and cluttering it up. Rotate what you are displaying throughout the event or as things sell.

- Create more space by going up. Bring boxes and shelves if you have a very small table so you can put things up rather than trying to fit everything flat on the table.

It's important to consider your target audience. At times, you may want to adapt your display, approach, and even your products, accordingly. For example, if you are going to exhibit at a show where only children shop for their Christmas gifts, lower your display for the children to comfortably see and display items priced on the lower end of the scale.

"How can you make an elegant, eye-catching table display on a budget?"
—*Michelle C., UT*

- Keep your color scheme simple. Brand to your company's colors if possible, and if not, just one or two choices that complement. Too much fuss and too many extras will make your display look messy, not elegant. People might look, it might catch their eye, but maybe not for the reasons you hope.

- Save some boxes. Turn them upside down and cover them with material that complement your tablecloth. Voila! You created height and beautiful display pieces to show off your items at no expense.

- Have a table cloth that covers to the floor on all three sides the customers can see. Your display will be neat and tidy while allowing you to store your extra bits under the table and out of sight!

- Borrow items for an elegant, eye-catching display until you are earning enough money to purchase your own.

Disappointment

I considered trying to figure out a way to put this section at the end. I'm a person who loves to focus on the positive. It bothered me to have a section discussing negative things in an early chapter of the book. However, on your vendor event journey, you *will* experience obstacles and disappointment. Possibly early on. Your very first event might wind up being one of your worst. With that in mind, I decided it is fabulous to have this section one of the first you will read. I hope that in reading the obstacles other vendors face, with suggested solutions provided, that when you face similar disappointments, you will be prepared to handle them in a positive way.

"Did you ever get frustrated with your business and feel like a failure? What kept you from quitting direct sales?" —*Dusty S., TX*

Soon after I joined my direct sales company, I found myself in the lowest, hardest place of my life. I believed that I was a failure at everything I touched and tried to do. I believe that direct sales, specifically the company and people I am blessed to be with, is what God threw to me as a life preserver, to hang on to and keep me from drowning. Yes! A thousand times yes, I got frustrated and felt like a failure in my business. I battled constantly with the lies in my head shouting that I had no idea what I was doing, that I was wasting our families' time and money and that this venture would implode and ruin more dreams and hurt more people. Myself included. That sounds a bit dramatic, but it is how I felt. What kept me from quitting direct sales can be summed up in two words: releasing GAS. Allowing my gratitude to re-focus my attitude on serving others. I call that "releasing GAS." Let your **G**ratitude for everything and everyone in your life change your **A**ttitude of thinking about the things that are wrong, and focus on **S**erving. Find ways to help others, build others up, and give, give, give. Give yourself through your time, experience, appreciation, and then keep doing it. I was so grateful for the people in the company that I joined and the ladies joining our team. I was blown away by the opportunity before me. I had no experience in direct sales, no idea what I was doing, and hadn't even begun to unwrap my success. What I did have was gratitude. It took my focus off myself and my problems and pushed me to find ways to help. Don't listen to lies whispering that you aren't good enough. Scream back, "Yes, I am! I have a lot of valuable things to offer!" When the going gets tough, allow yourself a good cry if you need it, release more GAS, and refuse to quit!

"How do I minimize chances of theft?" —Sara D., IA

- Stand up and stay near your crowd and products.
- Wear your money and your phone.
- Store additional inventory out of sight and out of reach.
- Avoid displays on spinning racks or racks that face the outside aisles you cannot see.
- Consider bringing help, to your event.
- If you must walk away from your booth, ask a neighboring vendor to keep an eye on it for you. Be willing to do the same for them.

"How do you avoid getting burned by unscrupulous event coordinators?"
—Allie B., MN

This rarely occurs, but has happened that consultants submit applications and payment for events that don't exist. Do your research. If you don't know the show and the coordinator, check it out before you send in your money.

Even when you do everything right, sometimes things don't turn out the way you hoped. I grew up loving and attending craft shows with my mom. Occasionally, she would book a table at a show to sell crafts she made, and I would go to keep her company. I enjoyed that time together, except for one disappointing event. My mom handmade the most adorable chenille teddy bears. Each was unique, with movable arms and legs. Her friends went nuts from the very first one she created and encouraged her to make a ton. They were certain she would sell them all! She spent an incredible amount of time lovingly making each beautiful bear. She booked a very well attended craft show and had a lovely display. Shoppers stopped to admire her bears. They picked them up, gave them little hugs, complimented her on her craftsmanship *and* the very reasonable price. Then, one after another, each put the bear back down and walked away. We were so excited by the praise, and we were sure her friends had been right—she was going to sell out! The hours went by, with the same compliments and teddy hugs, but no sales. By the end of a long day, I could have just cried. I never felt so sad for my mom. The bears were truly beautiful, and everyone said so, but not one single bear was sold that day.

I carry that story with me because as much as I was hurting for her, I remember my mother's amazing response. She focused on the joy in making the bears and wanted to please others with them. She placed several in various rooms of her home for family and visitors to enjoy, and when I became a mom, she gifted one of her special bears to each of my children. She didn't cry. She didn't get mad. She didn't even complain. She enjoyed her journey and her time with me at the show and found another way to bless people with her bears. She also didn't quit. She continued to find things she enjoyed making for gifts or to sell and she didn't allow that day to squash her love of crafting and craft shows. I'm grateful for the role model she was and continues to be for me. When your day comes, when you put your heart and soul into something and no one buys from you, I hope you'll be able to hold your head high, proud of what you have accomplished and keep moving forward. Consider this book my great big craft show bear hug from one direct seller to another.

—Shannon

E is for...
Evaluate

"Going through the motions isn't enough. It is the passion, energy, and excitement behind the motion that matters. When your heart peeks through, you change someone's experience of sales."
—Kalen Clark, Group Director, Steeped Tea

Evaluate

"If you didn't do well at an event, should you consider doing that same event again in future years?" —Sarah S. PA

I will give a show two chances before deciding it is not one I will return to for a while. The first year, a poor show might have been the result of weather, an important sports game that coincidently coincided, or the show being new and not established yet. After the second year, if the show remains poorly attended and with little evident results towards business growth, I will search for a replacement.

"How much is too much for a table fee? What determines a reasonable amount to pay for a space?" —Melissa S., OH

Too much is how much you are unable to recover quickly from losing if you do not make back your cost and earn profit at the show. Shows can range in price from free to thousands of dollars. They all have value to the vendors that book and attend them year after year. For your personal determination, ask yourself what you are trying to gain and see the chapter on "Risk" to help consider all the possibilities and make a wise business decision.

I encourage consultants that are new to the direct sales industry to start small. Small events, with even small crowds, can yield amazing results. You will have time to talk to and build relationships with the other vendors and the shoppers. Don't discount these little shows by assuming bigger must be better. Amazing things come in small packages and from inexpensive to book shows.

"Is it worth it to hand out catalogs liberally?" —April B., TX

No. Catalogs are usually tossed, the same as business cards. They are typically the most expensive piece of marketing in your advertising arsenal and should be reserved for guests at home parties or shoppers that specifically ask for one. I bring catalogs with me but keep them out of sight and only give them out when requested.

"What's the average profit from working at a craft show?" —Lydia S., KY

It's very difficult to give you an accurate average. Every show draws a different size crowd. Every company provides a varying profit margin. Every consultant works with different approaches and styles. Everyone has different costs to factor in. I have seen two people selling the same product at a show and one clean up and one go home in the hole.

Use the bonus show tracker provided to track all the details of your shows and you will be able to calculate your personal profit from events and determine which are the most valuable, for various reasons, to return to the following year.

Book Bonus:
Your Free Show Tracker Form: www.bit.ly/SuccessUnwrappedBookBonus

"Why do I need insurance? What kind of insurance? Should I have insurance if I only have a couple of shows a year?" —Carrie L., ID

You will not need insurance for every event, unless you personally choose to purchase it for all of them. Some events do require each vendor to obtain liability insurance for the length of their event.

If you only do a couple shows per year, you can inquire with those coordinators if they require you to obtain insurance. Some consultants prefer insurance to protect their business investment from theft or possible damage.

"What do you do if you need to leave due to emergency? Do you find the coordinator or just pack up?" —Christina V., MD

Whenever possible, make communication with the event organizer a priority. Event organizers do not appreciate vendors packing up and leaving early. In fact, some will ban you from returning the following year if you do. If you absolutely must leave an event early, do your best to let the coordinator know the circumstances and apologize.

"Does economic climate change how to choose shows?" —Vickie M., WA

Yes and no. This one is tough to evaluate in our industry. Frequently over the years, vendors have commented on why, due to the economic climate or current political elections on the horizon, sales are down, and we should expect them to stay that way for a while. But it's not consistent. Looking around the room and talking with more vendors, some are evidently busy and will comment they are having the best sales year of their career! Choose your shows wisely, with good business sense, no matter the current economic climate. All economic and other conditions being equal, vendors who adhere to the following will yield better results than those that do not:

- Remain positive even in difficult situations.
- Stand and interact with the shoppers.
- Work hard to continually improve their display and people skills.
- Show they care and give and take contact information.
- Use the contact information and follow up.

Those vendors will grow and build a strong, successful business faster than those who don't do those things, through good economic climates and bad.

Tip: Evaluate each show and keep track of its expenses, profit, distance, organizer contact information, notes of things you learned and more. This information will prove to be helpful when determining which shows to repeat and what changes to make the following year.

F is for...
Family, Fellow Vendors, & Follow Up

"While it's fun to sell at your booth, you'll find that your business grows better from the leads, bookings, and recruits you get that day, and after that day! Following up is the key!"
—*Nancy Ann Wartman, Director, Usborne Books & More*

Family

"Should I take my kids with me to shows?" —***Sarah B., PA***

Only you can determine whether you should take your children with you to events where you are working. Consider the following to help decide what is best in your circumstances:

- Ask the event coordinator. Some events have strict no children in the booths rules. Others will allow you to bring your children beyond a certain age. Some will permit you to bring any children of any age but do not allow them to leave your booth space without adult supervision. This is an important factor to consider if you were hoping they could walk around and browse the show and then realize they will be confined to only your allotted space for the duration of the day.

- Question how many people, children or not, are permitted in your booth. Some shows provide vendors with badges to enter and be worn and only a certain number per booth are provided. Extra helpers, or children, though permitted, may require a badge purchase.

- If permissible and you decide to bring your children, how will they be entertained throughout the day? Plan ahead and pack activities suitable for a small area. If you have electricity in your booth, you might consider bringing a headset and device to allow watching a movie or two.

- What size crowd is anticipated at the event? If your children are older, they might be fabulous helpers in any size crowd. If your children are younger, large crowds may require more of your attention and it may prove difficult to supervise young children and work the booth effectively.

- Bringing your children may result in not having to hire a babysitter. However, it may result in the show costing you much more than a babysitter would have if you buy them lunch and cave to their pleas of wanting to purchase things at the event.

- How do you handle multitasking? Will you be able to meet the needs of your children and the shoppers?

I have five children and have considered it a learning experience and wonderful bonding time to bring them with me to my events. One at a time. I have, out of necessity, brought several of my children on occasion, and it was not easy. The added voices calling, "Mommy! Mommy!" and desiring my attention or needing my help when I am working was stressful for me. The extra bodies in the confined space that stay, rather than a shopper that moves on, created a feeling of claustrophobia at times. For our family, bringing one or two of the older children, who can assist shoppers and are permitted to walk around the event unsupervised is what works for us.

I used to do all my shows by myself or with my mom, until my oldest daughter, Lydia, showed interest in coming with me. I don't make a habit of taking my young children with me, but thought I would give it a try. I looked forward to spending the time with her but was nervous too. How would she handle the long day, set up and tear down? What if the show was boring? I carefully choose the show Lydia would accompany me to. That show is now one that stands out as a memory we will never forget. Lydia was super helpful in setting up, and because of that we finished quickly. The show had a 'bird guy' and my daughter, enthralled with the parrots, went right over. At one point, she was holding six birds, including a white parrot! This was a once in a lifetime opportunity my daughter and I experienced together.

The best was yet to come. This event had a basket raffle, and my daughter spied an eighteen-inch doll that she knew she wanted to win. I gave her money to purchase a ticket. She stood and waited for almost two hours for the drawing. She was that excited about it! Honestly, my heart hurt a bit for her. It was a busy event, with tons of people there. Was she really going to win? About ten minutes before tear down, I was checking a lady out and suddenly, I *knew* she had won! I had no idea how I knew, but I could feel it, and teared up waiting for her to come back. Then came my precious daughter, carrying her doll, with tears streaming down her face. We still talk about that show two years later.

—Jessica Bish, Manager, Lilla Rose

Fellow Vendors

Many questions I have been asked, regarding fellow vendors, involve conflict or an uncomfortable situation. I am going to answer those questions but first focus on a few of my favorite things about fellow vendors.

- Fellow vendors often have experience exhibiting in a variety of events, and when asked, are willing to share their favorites and organizer contact information. They can provide tremendous learning opportunities for how to set up an attractive and crowd drawing display.

- Fellow vendors make great company during slow shows, and booth watchers for bathroom breaks. They are just like you—sharing something they love and hoping to earn some money or grow a business.

- Fellow vendors are people with stories. Some good and some bad. They have good days and bad days. You have an opportunity to serve them and meet their needs as much as your non-vendor shoppers.

- Fellow vendors may be your next best friend, customer, hostess or team member in disguise.

"How do you deal with the Debbie Downer neighbor?" —Sue G., TX

Attitudes are contagious. Good ones and bad ones. If your neighbor vendor is projecting a negative attitude, accept the challenge. It's *Survivor*, on Craft Show Island. Outwit, outlast, and outdo her negativity with your positivity. Refuse to complain or join in her negativity. Two outcomes are possible:

1. She will catch your positive attitude and the negativity will slow down or stop.
2. She won't. At the very least, you are doing all that you can to remain positive in an uncomfortable situation. Your shoppers will clearly notice the difference between you and your negative neighbor and it will wind up making you look even better.

"What should I do if I have a someone next to me who is not being an appropriate vendor? Rude, verbally aggressive, stealing business from your table, interrupting your sales to pull people to their table or encroaching on your space." —Holly B., PA

I make it a point at every event to introduce myself to my neighboring vendors. I inquire about their products or business, offer to be there to watch their booth later if they need a restroom break, offer assistance in carrying or setting big things up if appropriate, and verbally make them aware I am cautious not to overstep into their space. I ask questions such as, "Will this sign be in your way at all? I can move it if it might be." Starting each show with your best attempt to befriend the neighbors will avoid some potential conflict.

During such rude behavior, I would make every effort to keep my focus on the shoppers and not encourage the rude vendor to engage in conversation with me. It *is* rude to encroach on your space. But it's not worth fighting over. It's one day and one event. If you can, gently move your item back where you had it, or without attention, slide theirs back into their own space. If it will cause more trouble than it's worth, don't bother. Your interaction with the shoppers will far outweigh whatever you wanted to put in or utilize that encroached upon space for. I have never had someone purposely utilize part of my space, so I do not expect it will be a frequent problem for anyone.

If the event is over multiple days, ask the organizer if you can be moved to another location for the second day. Keep in mind someone *that* rude is not the type of person shoppers will want to work with. Do your best to keep smiling and offering great service to the shoppers in your booth.

"What do you do if one representative is hogging all the shows and not letting others have an opportunity?" — *Traci W., NY*

Most direct sales companies, in fact, all that I am aware of, do *not* have territories. Vendor events are on a first book, first vendor basis. It doesn't matter if you live closer to an event than another consultant. It doesn't matter if she has a lot of events already booked and you do not. If she has booked the shows, they are hers to do and enjoy. You will need to branch out into other areas and be willing to travel a bit further if necessary. In addition, consider that vendor events are but one means of sharing your products. If you truly cannot find events that are not already represented by your company, then focus on home parties, social media, and other avenues of unwrapping your success in your business.

"What happens when there are multiple consultants for the same company at the same event?" — *Stephanie A., PA*

Avoid this conflict by communicating well with the event organizer. Some allow multiple vendors from the same company. If you, or your company, are not okay with that, do not book a show with that coordinator if she cannot assure you will be the sole representative from your company.

If you find yourself at an event and there is another consultant from the same company already there, play nice in the sandbox. Your reputation and future success may depend on it. Asking the other consultant to leave, complaining to the organizer or anyone nearby, or letting it ruin your day will all yield negative outcomes. It is not an ideal situation for either of you. Respond, don't react, in the most positive way possible. On your show tracker, record the situation to avoid duplication next year.

I have worked hundreds of vendor events. Most fellow vendors have been a pleasure to get to know. I have made friends and appreciated their experience and insight on the world of craft shows. I see several year after year and we look forward to a hug hello, wish each other another great show, help one another as needed, and cheer on each other's success!

Tip: Consider assembling vendor goodie bags. Craft a little note wishing them a great show, pop a few little chocolates in the bag, and include a coupon for shopping at your booth. Walk around and hand them out with a quick "Good morning! Have a great show!" and you are well on your way to making some new vendor friends.

Events can be long and, at times, boring. You have no control over how many shoppers there are, who is spending money, or the snow that may be building up outside. One thing you can control is getting to know the other vendors. My spot was right next to a man and his wife who were selling homemade salsa, hot sauces, and these little burlap bags, "only five dollars for vendors." The story that went with the bags was worth way more than the cost of the bag. He held up this two-by-three-inch, well used bag, and told me it was for vendors only. It contained "be back dust," and he asked, "Do you know what that is?" I shrugged my shoulders and said, "No." He explained, "People will stop at your table. They spend time talking to you and looking at what you sell. In your mind, you are calculating what they will owe you for the items they have picked out and then it happens. They utter those four words: I will be back." He then reached into the bag, grabbed some invisible dust, and threw it into the air. "Just like that!" he said. "The dust disappears, same as your almost customer." We laughed together then and throughout the rest of that slow event. I had made a new friend and maybe even learned a new way to look at a vendor event disappointment.

—Jean Christian, Elite Status Presenter, Younique

Follow Up

"What is the best move for following up with my customers? What really gets great quality responses?" —Kim S., TN

I once found myself overwhelmed with a huge pile of receipts from shoppers. The purpose of the receipt copy is to follow up with and build relationships with the customers. However, one neglected stack from a craft show soon became two, then three, and so on. The pile was overwhelming and a daily, visual reminder that I was not doing what I was supposed to be doing! The stack was multiplying, and it became a temptation to toss the whole thing in the trash! I wouldn't have to see it and be reminded I'm a slacker if I just threw it away, right? My circumstances were overwhelming my reality. Thankfully, I did not cave and ditch the stack. Instead, I planned an attack!

When you feel overwhelmed with following up, or in any area of your business, Instead of giving up or giving in, try this:

1. Start by doing what's necessary. For my daunting receipt pile, what was necessary was simply contacting the **one** customer that had already emailed me and needed a response.
2. Next do what is possible. After I contacted that first customer, she was so grateful for my response and help, I didn't feel like such a failure anymore. I had about 45 minutes available and succeeded at following up with about 1/2 of the stack!
3. Suddenly, you will realize you are doing the impossible! It feels so good! That monster pile of receipts, was tackled in just 2 sessions! What

seemed overwhelming and impossible due to the circumstances was not nearly as hard as I expected!

Now, before you head off to call a few customers, let me mention one more thing. Take this truth, this principle of doing what's necessary, then what's possible and the ability to then conquer what you thought was impossible and multiply it out. What is your biggest, you think it's impossible, dream?

That dream come true is within your grasp! It's not impossible! Start with one necessary step, proceed by doing what is possible each day and soon you are unwrapping your success with dreams coming true! Here's to your impossible becoming your reality!

Follow up truly is where the fortune is!

Did you know that:

- 48% of consultants never follow up with their shoppers.
- 25% will make contact twice, then quit contacting their customers.
- 12% will contact three times, then quit contacting their customers.
- 10% will make more than three contacts to their customers.

Now consider this:

- 2% of sales come from a first contact.
- 3% of sales come from the second contact.
- 5% of sales come from the third contact.
- 10% of sales come from the fourth contact.
- 80% of sales are the result of the fifth to twelfth contact.

Let me put this as simply as I can. 80% of *all* sales are going to only 10% of all consultants. Yes, you read that right. That is why the fortune is in the follow up. Those following up, that 10%, are the ones earning a fortune! If you are not in that top 10% of consultants, willing to keep reaching out and contacting your customers, you will miss out on 80% of the sales available to grow your business.

Follow up by following these steps:

1. Collect contact information (see Customer Care for ideas).
2. Do not put the contact information sheets away.
3. Once home, place them on the chair of your desk, or an obvious place they will be in your way until you follow up.
4. Schedule a time within the next few days to follow up with every contact in the pile.
5. Do it. Follow up. Send an email, text, FB friend request and message, or call if that is their preference.
6. Do it again.
7. And again.
8. And again.
9. Make it your goal to be in that top 10% who are fantastic at following up and you will reap the rewards of being one of few receiving 80% of the sales!

On a scale of 1–10, 1 being the worst and 10 being the best, how would you rate your consistency and frequency with following up?

Consistency: 1   2   3   4   5   6   7   8   9   10

Frequency: 1   2   3   4   5   6   7   8   9   10

What are you planning to do about it?

_____

_____

_____

g is for...
Go Further & Giveaways

"Learning to make friendly conversations with perfect strangers is one of the best skills you can develop as a direct selling professional, and this will set you apart from others."
—Shelli Auger, Brand Partner & Trainer, Yelloow

Go Further

"What do you do to set yourself apart as a crafter?" —Stephanie M., OH

As much as you might love your product, in the pursuit of success in the sales industry, it doesn't matter what you sell. Don't get me wrong, what you sell might be amazing, something that you really love and are passionate about sharing with other people. But having a great product does not make you stand out from the crowd, attract people, build relationships, guarantee sales, or grow a business. To make the most of your event and truly unwrap your success, you need to go further than the other vendors are willing to go. Intentionally plan for you and your table to stand out as different and worth the shoppers' time and attention.

Some ways that you can do this include:

- **Merchandize.** One thing that always stands out and attracts attention to a booth is a crowd. When customers are crowded around, those passing by want to know what they are looking at. They assume it must be something worth checking out if others already are. To attract a crowd at your booth, stand in front of your display and straighten and move the items from one place to another. The appearance of someone looking makes it more likely that the next person will stop and start to build your crowd.

- **Stand up.** Be standing and willing to interact with those passing by your table. Greet them with a friendly hello, a compliment, or a friendly question about their day or purchases.

- **Be thankful.** Make it one of your goals at each and every event to be very friendly to the organizers and thank them for all that they do.

- **Stay positive.** Throughout the event, no matter the outcome or possible negative attitude of customers or fellow vendors, keep a positive attitude. This alone will help you shine and stand out as different from the rest!

- **Demonstrate.** If your product is one that can be demonstrated, be sure to take the time to show the crowd how it works. Allow your shoppers the opportunity to try the products themselves whenever possible.

- **Packaging.** If your budget allows, consider cute packaging for your customer's purchases. Include a thank you card or note inside their bag. Remember, every piece of marketing material or note you hand out should be clearly labeled with your business website and contact information.

- **Focus on the shoppers needs and wants, not your own.** As Bob Burg and John David Mann of Go-Givers Sell More say, "The truth about selling is that it's not about your product, and it's not about you—it's about the other person."

- **Follow up.** After you have put all of this thought and intention towards going further and providing such excellent service, be sure to follow up with everyone after the event. You have just made a great first impression and now it's time to continue building upon that foundation! See Customer Care and Follow Up for more details.

It often takes consumers until the fifth to eighth time that they are exposed to a product in some way to make a purchasing decision. How are you going to ensure that when these potential customers reach their fifth to eighth exposure that *you* are the one they are going to want to shop with? You need to build a real, authentic relationship with people whenever you can. You will stand out from the crowd as a person who focuses on people, not just products! Go further than other consultants are willing to go when you are with people! Follow up when you are not. You will be presenting yourself as a reliable person with integrity who cares about helping them. Your potential customers will grow to like you and trust you. When they are ready to buy, since you have done a great job and stayed in touch, they are much more likely to make their purchases with you. Not every sale will happen the first time a person sees your product, in fact, most won't. Try not to be disappointed when someone does not buy, but instead have the attitude, "However long it takes, I'll be here to help you now *and* when you are ready."

"To really go further in my business, what should I keep in mind?"
—Jessica B., PA

Working at craft shows is only one of many possible avenues and only one aspect of working your business. We are unwrapping your success through vendor events and providing a strong foundation for you to grow and build your business. Keep in mind that to succeed, reaching *your* goals and seeing *your* dreams come true, you need to complete the building project. Part of your intention at every craft show needs to include a plan of how you will continue the relationships started. Vendor events on their own will not unwrap your success.

Consider the following options to build upon your foundation:

- In home parties.
- Social media parties, groups, and other advertising opportunities.
  - Facebook
  - Twitter

- o Instagram
- o Pinterest
- o Blog
- Selling on the go.
- Customer care and follow up.
- Continual growth and development of your team.

Giveaways

"Should I donate a door prize?" —Kristi D., ND

- Some event coordinators require a door prize, or raffle item, and others do not. It's a good idea to ask when you register for the show, so you are prepared.
- If they do require one, they often set a specific minimum value requirement. This will help guide you in your selection.
- Select an item that is not size specific.
- Ask yourself, "What would I be excited to win?"
- Present it beautifully.
- Include your contact information and a reason for them to reach out to you. For example, in addition to their gift, you could include a coupon for 50% off any item up to a certain dollar value, expiring on such and such a date. If you are present when the winners are selected, ask if you can snap a selfie with the two of you and the prize they won to share in your VIP group. Invite them to join your VIP group (many will do it right there from their phones) so they can see their prize-winning photo!

"Do you think it is a good idea to have a give-away or raffle item in your booth?" —April S., WA

Yes, I do! The opportunity to win something is a great draw to your table that provides a fun way to expand your contact list. Be sure to ask the show organizers for permission prior to having a giveaway or raffle in your booth. See Customer Care for fun ideas and more information.

H is for...
Handmade & Helping

"Leaders lead all the time. If you want to lead, you can't sit back while someone else does it. You have to be the one to take charge."
—Conni Brown, Premier Team Leader, Posh

Handmade

"What if they won't let you sell your product because you don't make it?"
—Frederique S., DE

You have several options:

1. Find different shows that do not require the vendors to handmake what they are selling. You may need to expand your search and be willing to drive a bit further to attend vendor events.
2. Ask if you have at least some things handmade if you can sell your items that are not handmade. If the answer is yes, you could get your craft on if you really want to get into this show!

3. If the answer to #2 was yes, but you do not want to make anything, ask a friend who is a crafter if they would be interested in sharing a space with you.

"Does it help or hurt sales to combine selling my direct sales inventory along with items I handmake?" —Sara D., IA

- It will help your sales and increase opportunities if it grants you admission to great shows that you would not have been able to vend at if you did not have the handmade items.

- It could hurt your sales if your display is overly crowded, cluttered, or it's confusing and difficult to tell what you sell due to the mix.

- It could hurt your sales if what grabs the shopper's attention first is the craft item and it is something they are not at all interested in. They might completely miss the products on display from your direct sales company.

Tip: Always inquire with the policies and procedures of your direct sales company prior to combing any additional companies or items in your booth, handmade or otherwise. Some companies prohibit sharing a table or booth with their products.

"How do you answer the question, 'Did you make these?'? It seems like it turns people off when I tell them I didn't." —Rebekah C., FL

If a shopper came to a craft show expecting or at least hoping that they were shopping with crafters who personally made everything that they are selling, then you might be right. It might turn some people off when they realize what you sell is not handmade by you. I wouldn't let it upset you. They just had unmet expectations that you are not responsible for. What you are responsible for is projecting the best you that you can throughout this interaction. Smile and say, "No, I'm a consultant and get the pleasure of enjoying and selling these amazing (insert product)." There is no need for you to justify or rationalize your right to be there. If they are turned off, remember the "be back dust" and let their disappointment fly away with the dust.

Helping

"Should we focus mainly on growing our personal business, or helping others within our companies?" —Jessica B., PA

Did you ever hear the story of Punchinello and his boxes and balls by Max Lucado? Punchinello is a wooden person, created by the Maker, Eli. One time, he and the other wooden people became obsessed with collecting boxes and balls—who had the most, who had the prettiest or the most expensive. Towards the end of the story, the characters upped the ante. They raced to see who not only had the most boxes and balls, but who could be at the highest point in the village while holding them all. They pushed, shoved, and ran for the mountain top.

In the story, the illustrations show the wooden people stepping on one another, crashing into each other, knocking each other over, and boxes and balls tumbling everywhere! Punchinello was, himself, so busy watching what others were doing, and his arms were so full, he wasn't even on the right path! None of those wooden people reached what we would consider a mountain top experience. Or what you might call success.

It reminds me a lot of what happens when consultants are busy comparing themselves to others and trying to one up each other. Feelings are hurt, "balls" are dropped, people go off course, and at the end of the day, none of those consultants succeeds in reaching her goals. Stop wasting your energy on struggles and strife trying to beat others to the top.

Instead, focus on being the very best *you* that you can be and on helping and serving others—customers, hostesses, and team members. Build personal relationships with them, meet their needs, and provide such top-notch value with every interaction that they will start raving about you to everyone they know. Along your way to success on that mountain top, you could even help someone up who's been knocked down carrying too many boxes and balls and racing against the others.

I is for...
Intentional

"While sales are important to your business, if all you see are dollar signs instead of individuals, then your intentions are visible, and your opportunities limited."
—*Becky & Kevin Preece, Scentsy Independent Super Star Directors*

Intentional

"How can I be intentional with my time and actions while trying to grow my business?" — Heather M, OH

"I've got it! I'll buy this and do that, and I'll say such and such and everything will go just right and my business will explode!" Sound familiar?

Don't get me wrong, exciting ideas *are* exciting! And thinking through all you will do and say and being hopeful for the growth to come are all fantastic. However, there is a final step that goes far beyond the thinking, the planning, the buying, the preparing, the excitement, and the hope.

The final step is being intentional. Great ideas and things you might buy to enhance or grow your business are useless and a waste of your energy and money if you are not paying attention and making purposeful decisions when an opportunity knocks.

I learned this lesson when I took my littles to the zoo. They enjoyed a class while I planned to get some reading accomplished. I found a nice place to sit in the zoo cafe. Long before this zoo trip, I got excited about buying a display purse. I put thought into the purchase, as well as setting up the bag with my products on display. I imagined the attention and questions it would attract and was more than hopeful for the growth it would bring to my business.

But I left out that one final step. I wasn't acting with intention. Yes, I remembered to bring the bag to the zoo. Yes, I even remembered to put it up on the table, rather than the floor. But I wasn't paying attention. Plenty of ladies walked past my table or sat at their own near mine that morning. But all opportunities for sharing about my amazing products and company were wasted. As I was about to pack up, to my horror, I realized the bag had been sitting on the table backwards!

Being intentional is not always easy. Distractions and life put our mind on other things. The next time you are excited about your plan, what you have bought, set up, or gotten together for your business, be intentional. Pay attention and follow it through to completion so you can reap the rewards and excitement of actual benefits! Not just empty hope.

Success is more than possible. It's right there waiting for you to unwrap it! But the difference between success and failure could be as simple as paying attention and turning around your bag.

Are there any areas in your business, or how you work your events, that you feel you have not been paying ample attention? Jot down your thoughts here and how you intend to improve.

_____

_____

_____

J is for...
Just Do It

"Detaching from all outcomes allows anyone
the freedom to go for the 'no' every day."
—Emily Roberts, Diamond Plexus Ambassador

Just Do It

"What would I have to do to really be in the top with the super successful consultants in this industry?" —Kim F., OK

Every time you forget to collect contact information from a shopper, you just made a choice.

Each time you let another day pass and don't mail that package, return that email, phone call, or message, you just made a choice.

When you neglect to follow up and show appreciation and inquire if your customer is satisfied, you just made a choice.

You do have a choice! You can be in the 95% of sales people who make promises they often don't keep, don't put the effort in to follow up with their customers, and rarely show appreciation or care, or you can be in the top 5% of sales people who go the extra mile and just do it!

The effort you would need to put forth to be in the top 5% is, surprisingly, not a lot!

If you tell a customer you will mail their package on a certain day, just do it!

If you receive an email, text, or call, return it within 24 hours. Just do it!

If a customer purchases something from you, follow up! Ensure they are happy with their items, offer to be of any needed assistance, and express how much you appreciate them. Just do it!

That's it. Just do it.

That's not a very long list, but it *zooms* you to the top in the world of sales because so very many sales people "sell and so long" in one fell swoop! They see that one sale transaction as the be all and end all and miss out entirely on the customer relationship, referrals, and future business potential. Don't join the majority in saying, "Thanks for the sale! So long!" Instead, make a choice to invest yourself in being at the top of your game and the top of the list.

Be consistent, reliable and appreciative. Just do it!

Welcome to the top 5%!

K is for...
Kick in the Pants

"Popcorn is prepared in the same pot, under the same heat, in the same oil. But the kernels don't pop at the same time. Don't compare yourself to others! Your time to pop is coming!"
—*Chalott Nagai, Executive Director, Pampered Chef*

Kick in the Pants

"What do you do when you get discouraged and don't want to continue your business?" —Tracy B., MI

When most people come to a fork in the road, and are faced with the choice of turning left or right, they make a choice. Even if they hesitate momentarily, they can clearly see that standing still and going straight are not options. They evaluate, try to see or even guess whether turning left or right is the better choice. Eventually, they choose and turn. Coming to this fork in the road might make them uncomfortable. But if they truly want to reach their destination, they will turn. One way or the other.

When a person is at a fork in the road but they have not realized it yet, that is even more difficult. I have seen consultants trying to grow their business in direct sales standing at a very specific fork in the road. They are frustrated and not moving and they have no idea that they can't go both ways. They have not recognized that the choices they are making are the very reason they are not moving in any direction at all.

I call it the fork of "Pity and Progress." You must make a choice between the two. If you choose pity, you cannot have progress. If you choose progress, you will not be going down that road called pity.

Consultants seeking pity for themselves and the situation they are in don't recognize that by choosing to seek pity, they are ruining their own chances of making progress. By its very nature pity, a "woe is me" attitude, is headed in the opposite direction to progress and unwrapping your success. Pity, feeling sorry about a situation, doesn't change the situation, and keeps you focused on the negative—bad feelings, bad outcomes, and sometimes bad people. While your mind, attitude, and the words coming out of your mouth are focused on those things, expect that you won't be getting far in your quest for progress. Negative breeds negative. What you think about, spend your time talking about, dream about, and share with others makes a difference in your daily progress. You may be reading this book and wanting to unwrap your success, but your mind keeps going back to poor results from previous vendor events. You might be feeling sorry for yourself and your circumstances. If you make that choice, you've chosen the road called Pity. The great news is you can turn around! Your circumstances, or past vendor event experiences may have been less than desirable, but you can choose to refuse to allow that to hold you back from unwrapping your success and reaching your goals! Circumstances might slow you down, but don't allow them to stop you or turn you in the wrong direction. Stop complaining about everything that is going wrong, everything you think you can't do, and what you don't have as an advantage. It's not helping you. Focus on what you *can* do and what you *can* change! Take baby steps if you need to. Moving slowly is fine. Head in the right direction, down the road called Progress!

L is for...
Less is More & Location

"Don't pour more money into it! Pour more of you into it!"
—*Shannon Ferraby*

Less is More

"I struggle with trying to make it look easy toting all my displays, inventory, and overall presentation of the table. Is it just better to concentrate on less is better?" —*Pamela F., NY*

In so many areas of life, less really is more. We talk too much, we send emails that are too long, we have multiple hour meetings when half an hour might have accomplished as much. We use too many words when we are talking and writing when we could have said what we wanted to say in just a few words.

When we don't remember that less is more, much of what we say and do is ignored.

The same is true for your display at vendor events! Much of what consultants pour into and spend money on for their displays is at best ignored and at worst distracting the guests from where you want their attention to be.

Remember, less is more!

Don't make a bigger display, *make a bigger impact.*

Don't bring more stuff, *bring more focus.*

Don't pour more money into it, *pour more of you into it.*

To fully "own" the less is more concept takes preparation and decision making.

- Decide what is *essential.*

- Leave out anything that is irrelevant or distracting. I used to buy and use different colored table cloths for every season and holiday, decorations for the tables, and even had fake leaves and flowers going down my tent poles! Those weren't nice extra touches. They were extra money wasted, extra stuff to lug around. extra time to set up and take down, and extra reasons for the guests to not even bother coming to check out my products.

- Focus on remembering LESS is more!

    L—Let it go. Don't need it? Leave it home.

    E—Easy for everyone. Make your display easy on the eyes, approachable, and touchable with a consistent theme and colors.

    S—Stop and engage. Part of the essentials is having an attention grabber in your display. Something that will make them turn their heads and turn around to take a closer look, but something still related to your brand.

    S—Simple but powerful! Take advantage of your company's or your personal brand design, colors, and logo. Make it easy to see. It's like the Nike swoosh. If you see the swoosh, you know what it is. That's the result you should aim for in your display. Simple but powerful!

Location

"What is the best location for a booth. Middle aisle? Right side? End of an aisle?" —Rhashell R., IN

Location, location, location. That's what they say for real estate, right? When you rent a table or booth for a vendor event, consider that rented vendor real estate. Location *is* an important factor.

If you are displaying at an event for the first time, you may not have any choice in where the organizer places you. As a returning vendor, you can often request the space you had the prior year. Comment on your application if you would prefer the same space. When I have had good sales and interaction at an event, I do request the same space because it is easier for repeat customers to find me.

If you can choose your space, consider the following:

- A corner or end typically allows more space for you and shoppers.
- If you are in the middle, but need to demonstrate products, how will you get out to the aisle?
- Are there other companies with similar products attending? If so, request to not be near one another.
- Are there multiple rooms? If so, go for the largest. Some events have one main room, such as the gym of a high school, and some overflow class rooms. They are never as well visited as the main room.
- Are there outside doors? In cooler months, being near a door can get very cold for you and customers.
- If the event is outside, being in the same area as the other crafters is best.
- Are there food trucks or a room serving food? Being near those is usually a great spot.
- Some events have an upstairs and a downstairs. Not all events have elevators, so consider this if carrying items in and out. Going up and down stairs might be difficult for you.

- For outdoor events, choose shade over full sun, grass over concrete and flat over a hill.
- Whenever possible, it is best to be mixed, in the same room with the handmade item crafters, rather than in a room with all direct sellers.

I have three shows out of hundreds that are my absolute favorite and best shows. Best in attendance, best in sales, best in potential future growth due to the increased volume of people and possibilities through following up after the events. And because they are super fun shows with great music and atmospheres! I get excited to see old vendor friends and have a blast while making money and growing my business. One is a Scottish Games Festival. It draws thousands of people in their Highland Dress, bag piping their way all over the event. I love it! Well, I used to. I arrived early to set up but couldn't find my name spray painted on the grass anywhere. I didn't pay close enough attention and just assumed it would be in the same section I'd always been in, near all my awesome crafter friends. No such luck. I asked other vendors, asked vendor staff, and finally found someone with the organizers cell phone number and gave her a call. "Oh, you're up the hill, past the food trucks. You'll see a patch of grass, kind of in the center of the two roads." Sounded dubious. Back in the car I went, past all the crafters, crowd, and food trucks to the top of the hill. Lo and behold, there was a little patch of grass between two roads, and not much else. One lone other vendor was set up next to my orange name on the grass. There were only two of us up in that lonely location. When I spoke with my sole neighbor, she shared that the organizer told her that she had too many vendors in the other area and somebody had to be up here. That in future years she would be adding more and more to this area, and "Not to worry! The families go past that road to get their kits on and get ready for the parades." Trust me, neither of us were convinced or happy about our surprise location and segregated situation. I had a hard time staying positive that day. I had just booked my daughter's appointment to get her braces put on, needed $1000 for the deposit, and, based on experience, hoped this event would yield that much in sales. Alone and up in no man's land, I wondered if I would sell anything at all. The day dragged on and we were very slow. My daughter took several walks down to the vendor area and reported thousands of people milling about and shopping. We were lucky if a few came by every hour. When anyone did approach, I committed to giving them the best service I could and stayed positive. Sales were slow and low. I suspected if I ended with a few hundred in sales, that would be a lot. Around four o'clock, only an hour before the show was set to end, we had a rush! Nothing like the crowds down in the vendor area, but compared to the day we just had, it was an exciting hour! I went from one shopper to the next to the next and had no idea what I had sold, but just kept on moving. At five o'clock, when the day was over, I sat down to count before I packed up. Tears rolled down my cheeks when I put the last $20 in the pile and finished the count at $1000. It was a terrible location, the worst of the worst. The crowd was pathetically slow all day. The chances of meeting my goal seemed slim to none. Then, out of left field, an hour-long rush, hard work, and a good attitude saved the day. I sold as much in that one hour as I did in previous years down in the busy area. She put me in that spot again the following year. And the year after. I don't complain. "Location, location, location," unless you don't have a good one, then say, "Location schmocation! I'm going to rock this event anyway!"

— Shannon

M is for...
More or Less & Multiply Your Team

"This business is like a treasure hunt. You have to dig through a lot of sand to find the treasures. When you find the jewels, you will know it because they will shine."
—Melissa Dettmer, Independent Sales Consultant,
Vice President Sales Leader, Norwex

More or Less

"Should we always decorate our booths as much as possible?"
—Heather M., OH

As explained in the previous chapter, less is almost always more. However, you will find certain festivals have strict requirements on how you decorate, the colors permitted, holiday decorations required, and even some that require the vendors to dress in a style of clothing. Read the fine print on your vendor contracts and ask questions.

Such as:

- What size is my space?

- Will I be against a wall? In a corner? Have vendors on both sides of me?

- Do you require a certain color or style of tent?

- Do you require a specific color or length for tablecloths? (many require the cloth comes to the floor on at least 3 sides).

- Do you require holiday or themed items in my display?

Renaissance fairs and other "period events often require period style clothes, display items, and signs made of wood, not vinyl. Less is more, more or less, because, on occasion, you will have to veer from that mentality and adhere to specific guidelines to participate.

Multiply Your Team

"Should you focus on sales, bookings, or recruits at a craft show?"
- Erin S., IA

Yes, yes, and yes!

Vendor events are the perfect atmosphere for sales, bookings, *and* multiplying your team! At every event you do, you will meet new people who have not heard about the products and opportunities you offer.

Try sharing the business opportunity in some of the following ways:

- Display your business kit in all its glory.

- Include a sign in front of the kit so shoppers know it is "For sale. FREE business included with purchase!"

- Hang a help wanted sign, easily seen from a distance to attract those with job hunting already on their mind.

- Include an invitation in each bag to join you on an opportunity call where they will learn about the business and can ask questions.

- Have flyers about the business on the table with a note, "Looking for a way to earn extra income? Take one."

- Write with eyeliner on a mirror used in your display, "Are you looking at the next (company name) consultant?"

- Plant seeds in casual conversation while helping shoppers. For example, when someone comments how much fun you look like you are having, you can reply, "I am! Being a consultant with (company name) is so much fun! I can't believe I make a great income doing this!"
- Ask each person at checkout if they would like to take home information on the business opportunity. When they say yes, write down their contact information and commit to calling them in a couple days to answer any questions they might have.

Which of the ideas above will you implement at your next event to share your business opportunity?

_____

_____

_____

_____

What excuses have you been telling others (or more likely yourself), as to why you have not built a team? Do any of these sound familiar?

"I never bring up joining my team because I don't want to be pushy and offend someone."

"I'm just not lucky."

"My sponsor never trained me."

"I don't have time."

"I tried. I really did. Nothing works for me."

"I'm busy at events. I don't have time to ask people about joining my team."

These are common excuses I hear on a regular basis. Success comes after a lot of hard work.

Excuses don't work. You must do the work. Vendor events are hard work. Being intentional and sharing the opportunity to join your team is hard work.

N is for...
Never Negative

"As long as you continue to blame outside things, your circumstances are not going to change, and you're not going to hit your goals or realize success."
—Paula Ramm, Jr. Executive Director, Lilla Rose

Never Negative

"What should I do if the show is slow or there are no customers?"
—Holly B., PA

- Mingle with, sell to, and share opportunities with vendors.
- Relax and enjoy your day.
- Discuss what other shows vendors love and collect information.
- Organize your display and items.
- Spend quality time with any shoppers that do attend.
- Remind yourself often that even one shopper has a circle of about 250 people in their life and could result in amazing growth for your business.

- Go live on FB and share the event for locals who could stop by.

- Shop from the vendors for any gift needs you have coming up.

- Be sure to make notes on your show tracker form to help determine if you should give this show another try next year, or search for a new one.

Bonus Show Tracker: www.bit.ly/SuccessUnwrappedBookBonus

I cannot promise you that you will sell out, that you will have the best spot in the event, that your vendor neighbors will be friendly, the weather will cooperate, or that customers will even show up. As a vendor, there is always a level of risk involved when you sign up to participate. There are many factors involved that you cannot control. You should be aware of them and with a business mindset weigh the risks prior to signing up and paying for a space. Once you have secured a space, you have only one element that you *can* control. You. You control your attitude throughout the day. You can be that one vendor who is smiling no matter what, who thanks the organizer for her hard work, who doesn't complain even when the circumstances are horrible. The one who is pleasant and helpful to the shoppers and vendors around them and who doesn't pack up and leave early in a huff. People are watching what you do, listening to what you say and how you say it. As professionals in the direct sales industry, we need to be alert to the attitude we are projecting at all times. Be sure that your words, your actions, and your body language line up to a fantastic personal and business policy of Never Negative. You will, without a doubt, stand out among the crowd as among the very best!

Every action creates a reaction. Sometimes we call it the ripple effect. Every choice you make, every direction you move in, creates a ripple. A common way to visualize this is by watching a pebble drop into a body of water. It's just a small pebble, being dropped in one place, but has a huge ripple effect on the water all around where it was dropped. In the same way, the actions you take and the words you speak at your vendor events can have a ripple effect on other areas of your business and people around you. What type of ripple will you create at your next event?

Are you worried? Rather than drop that worry pebble into the pond and create a ripple of negativity, try dropping a pebble of peace Write a list of all the good things happening or that could happen from this event and everything you are thankful for.

Are you in need of more money but sales have been slow? Rather than drop that fear of finances pebble into the pond, creating a ripple of uncertainties and inactivity, try dropping a pebble of productivity and moving forward in the right direction. Pick one thing. Just one thing that you can do for your business and do it. That one small pebble of productivity will create a ripple and get you moving towards meeting your financial needs.

Are you overwhelmed with areas you feel you are not good at? Don't drop that "woe is me" pebble into your pond! Instead, drop a positive pebble by focusing on what you *are* good at.

As you drop peace instead of worry, productivity instead of inactivity, and positive instead of negative, you're creating a ripple that will go far and wide towards great show days and unwrapping a lot of success in your future!

O is for...
Others First

"When you care more about others and their success and wellbeing, your own success will be abundant beyond imaginable. A servant attitude is the key to it all."
—*Carly Reeves, Black Status Level 2 Presenter, Younique*

Others First

"Should I focus on myself or others while building my business?"
—*Cathy T., NJ*

When you consider other's needs ahead of your own, not only will their needs be met, but your business will grow and prosper as well. You can't approach your events with the mentality of, "Okay, I'll put other's first so I can come out on top!" That motive would come through loud and clear!

Instead, try to ask questions, get to know people and their wants, needs, and desires, and then consider how you might honestly be able to help them, or direct them to someone who can.

Other's first applies to customers, organizers, fellow vendors, potential hostesses, team members and more! An example of "more" might be a consultant who represents the same products in the same company but is not on your team. By remembering others first, you are conscious of offering to help them, if you are able, and most certainly would never do anything to take away their customers or any other opportunity they have established.

You have a choice to make.

And your decision can have a profound impact on your level of success.

Do you see the world and opportunities around you as limited? Where you feel you must compete with others because you feel pressured, as if there are not enough customers to go around?

Or do you see an abundance of potential hostesses, customers, and team members?

You must choose how you will see the world and the attitude you have about others.

Having an attitude of abundance and recognizing, as the great Zig Ziglar says, "There is plenty of room at the top, just not enough room to sit down," helps you to work hard, stay focused, and gives you freedom to put others first.

Events are sometimes difficult for me because I find it difficult to approach strangers. It's a lot easier for me when I focus on caring for the women at the event. I make friends with the other vendors and help them as I can throughout the day, and also listen to and care for potential customers that stop by. Taking the focus off of me is key!

—Heather Mason, Director, Lilla Rose

P is for…
Payment & Packing

*"Success is never overnight. But even a bucket can
be filled drop by drop with enough time."*
—*Michelle Withers, Creative Success Systems*

Payment

You should expect at vendor events that most shoppers want to walk away
with their purchase in hand. Though they are likely to have some cash on them, it
is typically needed for their coffee and donuts. As many as 50% of your paying
shoppers will prefer or need to pay with a credit card. If you are not able to
accept that form of payment, you very well might lose that sale. The odds of
them going home and ordering online are slim. Not impossible, just not
something you should bank on. Be prepared to find a way to accept credit card
payments for purchases. There are card readers available from a variety of
companies that will work with your smart phone or iPad with a cellular or wi-fi
connection. Be aware that though you often do not have to pay for the card
reader, you do give a percentage of each purchase to the card reader company.
The increase in your sales, by accepting credit cards, will far outweigh the fees

you pay for the ability to do so.

"How much cash should I take with me?" —*Sara D., IA*

$100 in cash, with $40 in ones, $30 in tens, and $30 in fives has always been ample to begin even my largest of events.

"When at a vendor event, should I risk accepting personal checks or should I stick to cash and/or credit cards? If I do take checks, what information should I make sure is on the check?" - *Tracy B., MI*

When accepting checks, I make sure I have their phone number, email, and address. Checks are a bit riskier than cash and card payments so you will need to determine if you are comfortable with the risk that a check could bounce.

"What is the best way to organize checkout?" —*Sheila D. NY*

My favorite tip to handling checking out your shoppers, especially if you are working the event on your own, is to wear your checkout station. Find or make an apron with two large front pockets, and one inside pocket with a zip for stashing larger bills. Keep your order forms on mini clipboards with pens attached, cash for change, your phone, and card reader for credit card purchases and your calculator in the pockets. You can even put in a few bags that have whatever marketing material you are providing already inside of them. If they won't fit, find a way to keep the ready to go bags accessible without having to go behind your table. A little stand or corner of a table behind a display works well. Hand a ready shopper the clipboard with order form and pen on it to complete, and while she does so, you continue to help other shoppers.

"Is it better to individually price each item or have a price list somewhere visible?" —*Sarah S., PA*

Both systems work well, as the goal is to ensure the shoppers can easily see the prices. Some are too shy and might want what you are selling, but because they couldn't see a price, will walk away without making the purchase. To make it easy for everyone, also display a sign that shows what form of payment you accept.

Packing

"What's on your list of must haves when setting up?" —Loree H., FL

- The big stuff
  - Tables
  - Tent and side panels, weights or other tie downs (gallon jugs of water or sand help in a pinch)
  - Hammer or mallet for pounding in tent stakes
  - Stool for shoppers or leaning on when you need to take a load off for a few minutes
  - Inventory
  - Foldable cart on wheels
- The medium stuff
  - Signs for the table and standing ones for better attention
  - Tablecloths
  - Display racks
  - Mirrors, if applicable
  - Boxes to turn upside down for creating height
  - Scarves, material, or cloth to cover boxes
  - Credit card reader and phone or device with cellular connection
  - An extra credit card reader. They sometimes stop swiping well and an extra is very helpful.
  - Extra battery packs for your phone or device.
  - Cash for making change
  - Bags stuffed with marketing supplies for shoppers
  - Extra bags and marketing materials in case you run out of the stuffed bags
  - Clipboards with order forms to give and get contact info
  - Plugs and extension cords if you have electricity

- o Gift bags or gift wrap for special occasions
- o Donation or basket for raffle if required
- The small stuff
  - o Breath mints
  - o Deodorant
  - o Hand cream
  - o Sunscreen
  - o Chapstick
  - o Feminine products
  - o Layering options to stay cool or warm
  - o Gloves in cooler weather
  - o Extra pair of shoes if you might have to walk across wet grass in the morning to set up.
  - o Sunglasses
  - o Tape
  - o Bungee cords
  - o Zip ties
  - o Money for food and for shopping, so you don't spend your earnings or more than you want to.
  - o Pens
  - o Calculator

"I can't believe it! I can't believe you are here! You have *got* to show me what these things are and how they work!" exclaimed a new shopper as she practically ran over to my booth. She had been walking down the center of the aisle, with no intention of heading in my direction, when my large, stand-up banner caught her attention. She recognized the Flexi clips on the banner and immediately rushed over to talk to me. "My son gave me one of those things for Christmas last year! It is so beautiful, and I really do love it, but I had no idea what it was for or what it did, so I hung it from the rearview mirror in my car." At this point, we were both laughing. She couldn't believe what she hung in her car for an entire year, thinking it was a decoration, was a hair clip! I was very grateful I had packed my large stand-up banner for that show. It's a great attention grabber!

—Shannon

Q is for...
Quality Time & Questions

"You never know who is going to be your next leader, so talk with everyone like you're going to see them again and again."
—Nancy Ann Wartman, Director, Usborne Books & More

Quality Time

"How can you manage to have quality time with your family members while managing a household and running a business too?" —Heather M., OH

Let's unwrap how to make the most of every workday and event and go to bed at night satisfied with that day's accomplishments!

"What gets scheduled is what gets done," says Michael Hyatt, founder and CEO of Michael Hyatt & Company. Utilize a planner, calendar, poster, dry erase board, an app on your phone, or scraps of paper if that's all you have handy. Pick a time to get your work done, write it down, and use the time wisely. When you are working, work. Commit to a solid 45 minutes to an hour at a time and race the clock to see how much you can accomplish in that scheduled block. You might like scheduling one day to research events, one day for booking events, one day for getting organized for events, one day for follow up, and, of course, you will have scheduled time for the actual events and any home parties you have coming up.

Like many of you, over the years, I have tried multiple planners and systems to get and stay organized.

I have found two fabulous options for you to consider:

- The one I am personally using and absolutely loving is the Full Focus Planner, created by Michael Hyatt. His daily big 3 and the aspects of the planner have truly revolutionized my ability to accomplish tasks and complete projects.

  Your planner purchase includes exclusive access to a series of short videos where Michael Hyatt will personally coach you on how to use each element of the planner. With these insightful tutorials from your Virtual Mentor, you'll be achieving purposeful tasks in no time! Visit www.fullfocusplanner.com to order or for more information.

- Belinda Ellsworth has designed and produced a planner that specifically meets the needs of direct sellers! Check out her planner and other training resources at www.stepintosuccess.com

One secret is taking care of things right away by striking while the iron is hot. There are days when you are on fire with ideas! When the ideas are flowing? When the fire is burning? When there are events available to book, customers and leads to follow up with, and other things to be done, you need to strike! Knuckle down and make time for it!

There won't be extra time. You must make the time!

You can forego a few things on your other lists to focus on your business while the iron is hot!

Creating great, daily habits and being willing to strike while the iron is hot is one of the secrets to managing home, family, events, and business in general, unwrapping success along the way.

Questions

"I'm not good with chitchat. What should I say to customers who approach my table?" —Marie S, PA

You have only one shot at making a first impression, and that impression can make or break your business relationship. You don't need to be good with chitchat or talk about yourself. Ask quality questions for an easy and helpful way to ensure your first and continued impressions are great ones! Put your focus on the shopper.

- What do they like?
- What do they need?
- What do they want?
- How are they doing today?
- Who and what are they shopping for?

We are talking simple questions. Nothing crazy or out of the box here. Be sincere, caring, and honestly interested in them and how you might be able to help them. Will every interaction result in a sale? No. But that shouldn't be your goal. A sale is a dead end if you are not intentional about continuing that relationship and developing that shopper into your customer. Start your relationship off the best way possible by asking questions. This shows the shopper that you care about them and you are on your way to building that long lasting relationship. With quality care and questions like that, this shopper is more likely to become your committed customer, hostess, or team member

R is for...
Register for Events & Risk

"The things that we are most fearful of are actually the things we must do in order to live out a dream."
—*Emily Chandler, Founding Star Director, Keep Collective*

Register for Events

"How do you find and book shows? And what determines a profitable show?"
—*Coral P., MO*

Time for a reality check. If you want to build a successful business working at craft shows and other vendor events, you must accept that they will not all be in your backyard. I travel at least an hour to every show I do, and finding the events is not always easy. Here are some tips to finding shows and important things to consider when booking them.

- **Google.** I suggest putting your finger on your town, on a map, and then draw a circle around it, about an hour in any direction, or however far you are willing to drive. Use those city/town names in your search. Here are some key words to combine with the city/town names to search for events in your surrounding areas.

- o Craft shows
- o Vendor event
- o Festival
- o Christmas shows
- o Bizarre
- o Holiday market
- o Expo
- o Art walk
- o Expedition
- o Spring fling
- o Fall festival
- o Trade show
- o Art & Craft show
- o Artisan fair
- o Holiday boutique
- o Farmer's Market

- **Booklets.** Some states and regions have craft show booklets that you can purchase. These booklets typically have the date, location, organizers' names and contact information, cost of show, and other pertinent information of shows in your region. To find out if there are any booklets like this where you live, try a Google search, and ask fellow vendors if they have or have heard of such a booklet.

- **Fellow Vendors.** Asking other vendors is my favorite way to find out about other show opportunities. You can typically find out not just what others shows are out there, but which ones are the great ones! Whenever you have the opportunity, chat with other vendors about their favorite and most successful shows. Ask why they return to certain events and ask them to share the contact information for the organizer if they have it.

You will develop relationships with the vendors, see them at future shows, and continue to be a great event resource for one another.

- **Newspapers and flyers.** Craft shows, festivals, and other vendor events are often advertised in town's local newspapers and signs displayed in local libraries and post offices. These options will help ensure you don't miss opportunities right in your neighborhood.

Once you have located at least one show you would like to register for, your first step is to contact the show coordinator. Bigger shows may have a website with a registration link, but most often you will email the organizer and request a registration form.

"How far would you drive for a vendor event? What information would you use to make that determination?" —Sarah S., PA

I drive about an hour each way for almost all my events. I am willing to travel a bit further, but the requirement for me is that I can drive home after the event. Unless it is a huge, multiple day expo, I do not want to add hotel costs to my list of event expenses. Therefore, my personal determining factor is if I'll be comfortable driving that distance in the morning to the show and again at night for the way home.

"What questions do you ask the organizer to see how the show will go traffic and sales wise?" —Judith K., TX

While emailing with the organizer, you should ask questions to determine if this is a good show for you to book.

- How many years has your show been around?
- In what ways do you advertise for the show?
- When do you start advertising?
- Do shoppers pay to get in to your event?
- What is your average attendance?
- How much is a booth?
- What size is the space?

- Is a table included or do I bring my own?
- Is a raffle prize or a portion of my proceeds donation required?
- Can I set up that morning or am I required to set up the day prior to the show?
- Are there any other costs I should be aware of, such as electricity or parking?
- Is there already a representative from my company booked for this show?
  - If there is and your company allows multiple consultants to register for the same event, ask: Do you allow multiple consultants from my company?

If you are happy with the answers, request an application.

Complete the application and turn it in with your payment.

You will need to have some money put aside in your business account to pay for your events.

You often cannot wait and book them at the last minute. The spaces fill up, especially at popular, well attended events. In addition, many shows do not allow two consultants from the same company. The longer you wait to submit your application and payment, the higher the likelihood that another consultant from your company has submitted theirs ahead of you.

"Do you only choose shows that have been around for many years or are first or second year shows successful too?" —Melissa S., OH

As a rule, shows that have been around for a while are better established and draw a larger crowd. Typically, if an organizer is not doing her job well—not advertising, not adding new and fresh vendors, not setting the room up in an appealing way for shoppers and vendors—then the show will fizzle out and stop happening. When you find an event that has been around for a while, they typically have a steady crowd of shoppers that look forward to and return to that show annually, as well as new shoppers who have heard about it and attend. There does often come a time, after many years, where it feels like an established, once amazing show has lost its pizazz. It may be that those established shoppers have all shopped with you several times. If your sales, contacts and growth are going down after attending the same show year after year, that is a good time to mix things up by trying another event, or just do something different at that one. Change up your display, create gift baskets with your products or ask for a different location.

New shows on the craft show circuit are likely to be a bit riskier of an investment. Even if the show organizer does a great job promoting the show, unless she is experienced and has run other successful events, there are a lot of learning curves and hurdles for her to get over developing a new show in a new venue. There are likely to be less vendors and no established shopper following. She may not have considered important factors such as advertising and not putting competing products next to or very near each other.

Though experience has proven that long standing shows draw a bigger and better shopping crowd, I always suggest consultants be willing to try newer events at least once or twice. It can be hard for direct sales consultants to find shows that do not already have a representative from their company. When a new show enters the circuit, you might want to grab it! Over time, that coordinator, if she is invested in the show succeeding, will get over the hurdles and learn what works and it may wind up being one of your most successful events.

"How do you know if your product will sell at a craft or trade show?"
—Susan M., OH

There is never a guarantee that your product will sell at specific events. If you sell makeup, you might book a wedding expo and assume there will be so many brides and bridesmaids that you are going to have a booming business day! Instead, the brides are all focused on veils and flowers and you are not nearly as busy as you hoped. Perhaps you would have never considered vending at a gun show. Try it! You may find that out of the box shows provide a reach to a new crowd you wouldn't have otherwise had exposure to.

"What are the best months to do craft shows? What are the worst?"
- Sara D., IA

- October and November are the two best months to be a vendor at shows.

- April, May, and September fall in at second best.
- June, July, August, and December are third.
- January through March are typically the slowest months for vendor events. The exception to this would be states that have farmers markets and other outdoor events year-round.

Risk

"What kind of risks are involved in starting your own business?" —Kim S., TN

Congratulations! You are a business owner. Owning a business comes with decision making, investment, and risk. I'm going to assume, since you are taking the time to read this book, that you are interested in growing your business and not being a hobbyist in the direct sales world. With that in mind, let's talk about your investment and risk working the event circuit and how to make sure you are getting out of the red and into the black and beyond!

- When evaluating show venues and determining if the returns will be worth your investment, first ask yourself these questions:
  - Why am I working in this business and why do I want to work at shows?
    - Is your why big enough and exciting enough to keep you going while you are in the red and working your way out?
  - What are the current market conditions of other similar businesses and other consultants in my company working at vendor events?
  - What are the current market conditions of the buyers at the events and in the areas where I would like to be a vendor?
  - How much time, money, and effort can I afford to invest?
    - Affording to invest means that if you sell nothing, you will be financially stable going home with your products you brought, ready to try again the next time.
    - Affording to invest means that you are not paying a sitter, for example, more money than you are likely to earn while at your

show, and then will be stuck without groceries if you don't make enough profit that day.

- Affording to invest your time means that you have other bases covered and can spend the hours required to prepare for the show, work the show, and follow up after the show.

o Consider short- and long-term investments that will be required and consider the ongoing investment needs.

o Once you sell inventory at one event, you will need to re-stock with part of the proceeds from that day's sales.

o What other purchases besides inventory will you need to work the events you have planned or are considering?

o What travel costs will you incur?

o How much could potentially be earned? Consider the length of time at the event, the foot traffic coming through, the available inventory you will have to sell that day, and previous shopping patterns at this show.

o What other benefits will develop besides sales?

- Consider bookings, team building, learning and personal growth, planting seeds, and developing relationships.

Being a business owner in the direct sales industry is a very *low* risk investment in comparison to other business ventures. Your initial financial investment is minimal in comparison and there is potential for a very fast return. Most business owners need to take out loans to start their business and most take between one to ten years before they can pay that off.

- A simple equation you can count on: The more money you invest, the more time and energy you will need to give towards earning it back. As the investment increases, so does the amount of time it might take to get back in the black. A consultant who invests $50 will not have to work as hard or as long to earn that $50 back as a consultant who invests $500 or $5000.

- Lead with your head, not with your heart. This is a business, so you need to treat purchases with that in mind. Evaluate if they are necessary and beneficial or if you just have the shiny object syndrome for newly released products or that new adorable swag that you don't *need* but would look so stinkin' cute!

- Lesson the financial risk of participating in events by borrowing what you can until you are earning enough profit to buy your own. Your company might sell a lovely tablecloth, branded with your colors, and that is optimal eventually. For now, just borrow a tablecloth and look forward to adding the branded one when it doesn't put you more in the hole.

- A great rule of thumb to get you out of the red and into the black while minimizing the risk factor is to earn before you spend. If you really want to buy something for your business, get out there and work! Sell a few products and earn the money for that additional purchase.

- As you sell and start to earn, pay yourself and then pay your business. Invest back in so you are never again at ground zero starting over. Spending everything in your pocket from a show, instead of investing in a portion back into your business, is like falling into business failure quicksand!

- Open a separate account for your business. Keep track of purchases, fees for your shows, other expenses, and the money you have earned. This provides an easy visual to determine how your business is prospering financially.

- Go big! A profitable business is what everyone wants. Profit simply means you have taken in more than you put out. If you spent $300 and ended up with $301, even though that is technically in the black and profit, it is not anywhere near enough to be considered a healthy earning. Go big! Aim for well beyond the black!

Owning your own business and being a vendor at events is risky business. Now that you have evaluated the costs and potential return, ask yourself, "Am I ready to work this? Really work this and work towards being beyond the black?" Set goals. Long-term, amazing, big goals. And small, stepping stone goals to help you along the way. As you are working hard, each month you will see progress and increase in the amount you are out of the red and into the black, and even way beyond!

S is for...
Setting Up & Sharing Shows

"Don't let the beliefs of others guide your business.
They are not driven by your 'why' each and every day."
—*Jessica Fogarty, Unit Organizer, Princess House*

Setting Up

"I'm doing an outside show, how am I going to set the tent up on my own?"
—***Jessica B., PA***

Here is some great news! Depending on where you are in the country, for most of us, there are only a few months of the year where a tent is needed for the outside craft shows and festivals. When you are purchasing a tent, remember that you might be going on your own sometimes. More important to me than setting it up, is can I get it in and out of my car on my own? Once I get the tent from my car to my allotted space, which I can do by myself, but I am sweating and struggling, I *cannot* set it up by myself. Maybe you are stronger than I am. I would bet most you are. But here I am, many years into doing outside events requiring a tent and I can confirm that never once have I been stuck trying to put my tent up or take it or take it down by myself. Many times, a fellow vendor or their spouse will see me starting to have a go of it on my own and they will offer their assistance. Other times, no one is near by or no one offers, and I need to ask for help. Just ask. I've never been turned down. Once or twice, I have offered to exchange product for their help. I remember once, there were two men working in a food truck across the way from my space. I went over and offered to let them both pick out a beautiful gift for a woman in their life if they would please help me set up and break down my tent after the show. They thought that was awesome! They were happy to help me, and both went home with a gift for their wives.

Sharing Shows

"Should I work events by myself or take someone to help?" —*Sara D., IA*
"How do you split sales when working with a fellow consultant?"
—*Judith K., TX*

Sharing a show with another consultant might be a terrific idea! Or, it might not. Let's unwrap why people want to share an event with another consultant in the first place, the pros and cons of doing so, and practical tips for how to make it work should you decide it's the best option for you.

- "It's a big show you know!"
  The most common reason consultants in our industry desire to have help, or another consultant to share the show with them, is because they are afraid they will not be able to handle it on their own. The idea of someone there to help you is very appealing. You might be nervous about your ability handle the crowd and are hoping that sharing the show with another consultant will calm your fears, solve your perceived problems, and hey, it might be a whole lot more fun with a friend!

- "I have to pay for parking, the booth fee, electricity, marketing supplies, inventory and let's not forget my coffee and lunch! Phew! This day could cost me a fortune!"
  The second most common reason sales representatives desire to share an event is to help cover expenses.

- The third reason I've seen consultants share events is because someone asked them to or they've seen others doing it that way. Learning from other's examples can be wonderful.

To share or not to share? That is the question!

Let's look at the pros and cons of sharing an event with another consultant using the list of potential reasons one might consider sharing in the first place.

- "This shows brings in hundreds (sometimes thousands) of people!" If this is your concern you are intimidated by the size of the event and the crowd attending.

  o Pros: If you share the event, you can maximize the amount of people you serve. One consultant can be drawing in the crowd while the other is helping individuals. One can demonstrate products while the other handles checkout.

  o Cons: If all goes well and the extra person is truly helpful, you may have a larger crowd to serve and sell to. However, you now also will have half the sales, and half the future customers, hostesses, and team members. In addition, you can't control how the person you are sharing with interacts with the crowd. They might be amazing! But they might not be.

- "What if I'm helping one customer and lose another because I was too busy?" If this is your concern you are worried about spreading yourself too thin and losing potential sales.

  o Pros: Assuming the person you share with works the crowd well with you, having them there can really help with this concern. While you are helping a shopper pick out "just the right item" she will see that new shopper approach and tend to their needs.

  o Cons: If your assumption that this person will work well with the crowd turns out to be false, then you will not only be losing shoppers when you are very busy, but you run the risk of being frustrated that you are doing all of the work and she is not helping. Clear communication of expectations can go a long way to prevent this from happening.

- "Who is going to watch my booth when I have to go to the bathroom?" Yeah, that's a good point. You are going to need to do that. If this is a concern of yours, you are either worried about someone stealing from you or losing customers in your absence.
    - o Pros: If you share, you can take turns with bathroom, coffee, lunch, and walk around breaks. It sure is nice to have a few minutes away sometimes. Of course, if it's really busy, sometimes you just can't peel yourself away from the excitement!
    - o Cons: The only potential con in this area is if the person who is supposed to be helping and sharing your show keeps taking all the breaks and is having a good ol' time while you are doing all of the work. Communicating prior to the show how breaks will be divvied out can prevent that from happening.
- "Don't I need a person just to handle check out?" If you have asked yourself this question, then you are concerned that you won't be able to do everything all by yourself.
    - o Pros: Though you do not need a separate person just for checking people out, sharing the show provides extra hands. You know what they say, "many hands make light work." Or, in this case, "many hands makes sure someone can checkout and collect the cash!"
    - o Cons: The confusing part with sharing a show and checking out can be determining who gets the sale and who collects the money. This can be simple if you plan and everyone is on the same page.
- "What if someone steals something? I can't be busy helping *and* watching people!" It is a common concern that theft may result in you not making a profit, or as much of one, at the show.
    - o Pros: Sharing the show with another consultant provides an extra pair of hands to do the work, feet to do the standing, and eyes to do the watching. But even with two or three of you, if someone is set on stealing something, they are likely going to accomplish that anyway.
    - o Cons: There is no con to having someone share the show with you when it comes to concerns about theft. However, since one concern of

theft is the fear of not making enough money, do look back to the first concern listed in this section. Yes, you will have two sets of eyes helping to prevent theft, but you have given up half of everything to maybe hang on to the *one* item *one* person *might* have stolen.

- "It's going to be expensive! I need to split these costs!"
  - o Pros: Yes, sharing the show, when details are communicated clearly and your intention is to share equally, will split your costs. In addition to splitting the costs, your risk factor, if you don't sell well, decreases.
  - o Cons: Initial expenses are cut in half but your profits and future business growth is also cut in half.

- "She asked me to share the show with her, so I felt like I had to." You are concerned about hurting someone's feelings if you don't accept their offer.
  - o Pros: It should put a smile on your face to know that someone thinks highly enough of you to want to work an event with you. Maybe this is the start of a great business relationship. Since she asked you to share her show in this case, one pro is that someone else did the leg work of finding and booking the show. In addition, you will have the opportunity to expand your business to a new crowd and hopefully learn from and enjoy the time working with the other consultant.
  - o Cons: Just because she asked, doesn't mean you have to say yes. If you say yes to her offer, what are you saying no to? Consider whether her method of sharing shows is different than what you have in mind. Be sure to ask a lot of questions and be very clear on the expectations and plan before you commit.

Which of the above reasons are why you have or might consider sharing a show with another consultant?

_____

_____

_____

_____

Perhaps you don't have any of the above concerns, but have thought:

- "I see consultants sharing shows all the time. I figured that is just the way to do it"
  - Pros: Learning from others' examples is a great thing. You can attend shows and learn how consultants interact with one another and their shoppers. You can pick up great tips on set up, display, and sales and marketing techniques. There are a lot of pros to being willing to work with and learn from others.
  - Cons: If you share shows just because everyone else is doing it, you might be missing out on a lot of great opportunities. If you choose to share shows, do it because it's what you have decided and, after careful thought, that it is what is best. Learn from examples. Good ones and even bad ones and make wise decisions for your personal business.

Be aware that if you want to share a show, who you share it with is of great importance. Consider the following:

- Your brand and reputation are at stake at this event. You are in total control of *your* attitude, *your* approach with shoppers, and the impression of you and your business that *you* make on the guests. You are *not* in control of any of those things in the person you are sharing a show with. Be sure to choose a person you know well and trust.

- Share events with consultants who work their business in a similar way to you. Some differences might complement one another. For example, if they are more outgoing, they might do a great job interacting with the crowd while you take the quieter roles. Question their work ethic, their dedication, their commitment level, and their attitude. Is she a positive person and will she remain positive even in the face of a slow show or other issues that might arise? Choose wisely so the person you share a show with will compliment what you are doing and make it an even better event for everyone!

- You know who your friends are, you love them and have a blast hanging out with them. But this isn't a slumber party. This is your business. Will they work? And work hard? Fun is no fun if you get stuck doing all the work while they scoot around the show shopping and enjoying their day! It's also not going to be any fun to share a show with a friend who must be in control of everything and have everything her way all of the time. Choose to share a show with someone you can compromise with. Even something as simple as picking out a tablecloth could turn into a huge dilemma if the person isn't willing to work with you.

- Consider the financial cost. Can this person afford to share the costs with you and provide the necessary inventory? Is this person reliable and trustworthy with financial matters? These are important things to consider as you will be handling expenditures and income together.

If you have thought it all through, weighing the pros and cons, and have decided to share a show, here are my top three tips for two to tango together beautifully at an event:

1. Communicate
2. Communicate
3. Communicate

It is simply not good enough if *you* know what you want, how you want it, and then proceed in that direction. That is a train wreck waiting to happen. You can't make assumptions that the other party just "gets it" or you think certain things are obvious. Clear communication is the number one way to ensure, no matter how your show turns out, you and your show partner have worked well together and consider the day a success!

Here are ten important considerations to discuss and decide together prior to the show:

1. **The Display:** Whose decorations, display items, tablecloths, signs, etc. will you be using? Get together before the event and do a mock set up.
2. **Setting Up and Breaking Down:** Who is setting up? Who is breaking down? Make arrangements to get each other's things back if one takes them all home.
3. **Inventory:** Whose inventory will be put out? If both, how will you keep track of whose is whose? If only one person's items are on display, how

will the other consultant replenish their half of what sold?

4. **Hours:** Are you working the entire show together or working in shifts? Arrange all times and days.

5. **People:** Are either of you thinking of bringing other people to the event? A spouse? Children? Members of your team? Discuss this to eliminate surprises. A focused, no nonsense, "let's do this" consultant might not appreciate the surprise of your husband and young children hanging out in the booth with you all day.

6. **Shoppers:** How will you work the crowd? Will you take turns? Or will one person help shoppers and one check people out? Are the ones you personally sell to now your personal customers? I would warn you against that approach. It can cause a sense of competition to get to the customers first, or to work to get the big buyers.

7. **Marketing Materials:** I suggest prepacking bags with your own marketing materials and she doing the same. Then arrange them, hers, yours, hers, yours, etc. Do the same with the mini clipboards with order forms. When a shopper is ready to checkout, you grab the ones on top. By the end of the day, you'll have worked the crowd as a team and each have half the shoppers to follow up with.

8. **Working and Breaks:** Decide in advance how many hours each will work and when you will take breaks and for how long. Discuss things like standing versus sitting down at your booth. That might sound silly until you've worked a show where your legs, feet, and back were killing you because you felt strongly about standing and interacting with the guests and your show partner was sitting behind the table eating, reading, and playing on her phone for most of the event.

9. **Show Me the Money:** Who is going to pay the event fees, parking, and put gas in the car if you drive together? Break down every cost and discuss who is paying what. Plan who will bring change for shoppers paying in cash and how much. Who will accept the credit card payments? How will you keep track of the sales and be sure the profits are split fairly? Who goes home with the cash at the end of each night for multiple day shows? Nothing can ruin a friendship and working relationship faster than money trouble. Don't make assumptions.

10. **Evaluate:** Before the show even happens, agree on a time and place to evaluate the shared event. What worked well for you both? What could have gone better or been handled differently? Did you both enjoy working the show together? Be honest and try not to take things personally. This is a business. Be kind but be truthful. It would be far worse to act like it was seamless and wonderful and then the next time a show comes up your show partner can't understand why you keep trying to wiggle out of doing it together. Continue to evaluate after each shared show and decide whether you will continue to share shows in the future. Sharing one event doesn't have to mean you will always share every show.

If you want help but don't want to actually share or split your show, here are some ways you can meet the need for help without sharing:

1. **Hire Help.** If you can offer to pay a friend, family member, or even a fellow consultant, do so. Agree on an hourly rate or a percentage of sales in exchange for their help at your show. The same rules for great communication apply. Be very clear that you are asking to hire them, not offering to share the event. In addition, be very clear what will occur if the show is a bust and you do not make any or much profit.

2. **Bring a Helper for Free.** Perhaps you have a teenage child, niece, or nephew who needs to get some volunteer hours for school.

3. **Offer Team Training.** You can offer for consultants on your team to join you for a certain amount of time, in shifts, with the goal of receiving training. You have some help and extra hands and they benefit from your expert training in many aspects of working a craft or vendor event.

If you and your show partner sell different products for different companies, consider the following:

- Will the show organizer allow two companies' products displayed in the same booth or table space?

- Does either company have any polices that prohibit you from displaying your products at the same booth or table?

- Consider your available space. Is there enough room to create an inviting display with two companies varying products?

- Think about your company and business branding. Your display should be uncluttered, attractive, and inviting. Is that even possible if you mix multiple brands and items? Dog treats and delicate jewelry would not blend well, for example.

- Anticipate that one table in a booth will attract more attention than another. For example, a table placed at the front of the booth, in the pathway, always attracts more attention then a table on the side aisle. Who will get which table?

T is for...
Taxes, The Three S's, & True Colors

"Being authentic doesn't mean that you refuse to grow, or that you remain a victim of your biases, shortcomings, and inclinations. It means taking the correct actions to improve, becoming a better, more effective, truly authentic version of yourself!"
—Bob Burg, coauthor of *The Go-Giver* and *The Go-Giver Influencer*

Taxes

"Can I add sales tax to my item prices and have my prices whole dollar amounts?" —Carrie L. ID

For all questions involving taxes, sales and income, please contact a tax professional in your state. Tax requirements and regulations vary from state to state. Therefore, any advice I might give could be incorrect for your area or your personal situation. Sorry! But you'll thank me once you have reached out and have the accurate answers your business deserves.

The Three S's

"I really enjoy selling at my craft shows. Is it okay if I just focus on that and not the other stuff?" —*Jean C., OH*

The Three S's are Sell, Share, and Support. It is crucial to the growth and success of your business that you balance your focus and your time between these three very important areas. This truth applies whether you are holding a home party, utilizing social media to grow your business, selling casually on the go while living life, or representing at vender events. You must make a conscious choice to focus on each of these Three S's and then just do it!

The last thing you want is to catch a case of direct seller's intentional blindness! Intentional blindness is when a person fails to see something in plain sight. Selling, Sharing, and Supporting are all crucial elements towards unwrapping your success and reaching your goals with a thriving business. You can't afford to focus so heavily on one that you become blind to the others. Each of the Three S's represents a source of income and growth for you to unwrap.

- If you focus only on selling, as you can only be in one place at a time, your income has a lower ceiling.
- If you focus on only sharing, building a team, but don't sell, you are missing out on the highest percentage of commission offered in your company's compensation plan, as well as the opportunity to continually meet and build relationships with new people.
- If you share and sell but don't support your team or your customers, you will lose them and always be starting from ground zero.

Have you been focusing too heavily on any one or two of the Three S's and blind to other areas? Which ones?

_____

_____

_____

_____

Selling: Selling is serving by providing your fabulous products or services to others. To meet *their* needs, *their* wants, and *their* desires. You can't force anyone to buy from you, but you can provide all the needed information, benefits, and explain and demonstrate the solutions your product offers. While at your events you will find most shoppers prefer to walk away with their items that day. That's not to say that you will never have someone willing to place an order, but plan on having some inventory for cash and carry whenever possible. The guests attending a craft show came knowing what they were walking into—a shopping opportunity.

Sharing: Sharing is offering your business opportunity. Remember, you can't be everywhere at once. While you are working at one event, or busy with other aspects of life, your team members can be out working their business and you have increased your income with this additional team bonus compensation. You can share the opportunity to join your team everywhere!

- Craft shows
- Business groups
- Mom's & kid's groups
- Work
- On social media
- At home parties
- Social events and more!

Supporting: Supporting is caring for and providing guidance to your customers and your growing team. At any given point in your direct sales career, 1/3 of the people on your team are new, or coming. About 1/3 are there, or staying, at least for now. Some are actively working, some not. And 1/3 are going. They have quit or are planning to soon. With this rule of thirds in mind, you need to be consistently supporting the business you are building, or you run the risk of even more leaving, none coming, and the ones staying having no idea what they are supposed to be doing.

Consistent Activity = Consistent Results

True Colors

"What is your secret? How did you get to the point of making such a great income?" —Susan M., NJ

Think about the leaves on a tree. They look green most of the year, and that's what you see, but underneath are the leaves true colors. When you look at me, and other direct sales leaders, you might see what you equate to success and you see green: money. The money earned by being successful in this industry. Let's strip away what most of the world sees, the green, the money, and get down to the true colors of my success and what I believe are secrets to your future success!

The secret to my success is in giving and serving others and always letting who I really am, my true colors, show. The true colors are a way to help us remember what we should be focusing on, and it's not the green stuff!

The true colors of leaves, the pigments, that come out when the green is no longer the focus are; red, yellow, orange, and since eventually they all wind up turning it, let's include brown.

- **Red**: Red can remind you of a heart. One secret to being successful at events, and as a direct seller in general, is leading, giving, serving, and making decisions with your heart. Making decisions based on what is best for the other person, not yourself. When working your events, I challenge you to remember the red and help your shoppers based on what is truly best for *them*, not what is best for you. Though many sales cultures are riddled with competition, I propose a better approach is to create an environment of cooperation!

- **Yellow**: Yellow is a reminder of being a light. A positive, bright force in people around you. What can you do at your next craft show to bring a smile to others faces, to lift them up when they are down, to encourage, motivate, and help them see the very best possibilities in themselves. Rather than focus on the green (getting), focus on the giving. Not as a means to getting the green, but because it's your desire and your way of life! Don't give in to rivalry, instead, build relationships!

- **Orange:** Is there a spark lit under you about your company, the people in it, the products, and your business in general? I hope so! Orange is for the fire. For the passion for what you do that just explodes out of you. You are sharing something you personally love and are excited by how it can help and benefit so many others. It is such an explosively amazing opportunity you just can't keep it contained! You are on fire! Don't waste your energy on struggles and strife trying to beat others to the top. Instead, be on fire to serve and support. Your fire will spread and you'll find yourself at the top celebrating with all of those you brought with you.

- **Brown**: Brown helps us remember dirt. To truly unwrap success at your events and well beyond them for your business, you need to be a leader, not a boss. Leading by your own example of hard work. Willing to get your hands dirty. Model consistent activity, determination, digging deep and that even when you hit hard ground, you never quit! Rather than thinking of yourself as "higher' than others, desiring to earn money off of them and their work, be humble, helpful, and hardworking yourself.

Cooperation	not	Competition
Relationships	not	Rivalry
Serving and supporting	not	Struggling and strife
Hardworking and helpful	not	Higher than and haughty

For many of you, these things are your true colors already. All you need to do to unwrap your success is focus on these colors instead of the green.

Others of you might be thinking, "But I'm not like that! Not at all! I *am* working this business for me and I *do* want team members so I can earn more money from their sales. I *do* want customers because I am driven to earn that commission!" I have great news for you! If your true color, really is green, and that is what you are focused on and what others can see you are focused on, the great news is that deep down, even though you don't see it, you are made up of a mix of red, yellow, orange, and brown. If those colors do not naturally show for you, with focus and practice and determination you can *learn* to let those true colors show. The more you do that, the more it becomes natural for you.

I have more exciting news!

I believe that you should not show, or lead, with your focus on the color green, the money. You will not be able to fully unwrap your potential and success if your sole purpose, desire and goals are to make money.

But here's the coolest thing. When you show your true colors, you:

- give from your heart.
- let your light shine.
- burn with passion for what you do and share.
- do it all while getting your hands dirty doing the work.

The green comes back to you! The green is not the goal, but focusing on those true colors *does* grow you and your team and your business, and you will stand in awe one day at the successful business that has grown and how you are financially thriving. Not because you are so great. That's not the secret. Not because you are any better or smarter or more talented than others. That's not the secret either. Rather, it's because you took the focus off yourself and let your true colors show by focusing on giving, loving, helping, and serving.

My husband and I work the business together. We feel like Lilla Rose is an extension of ourselves. For us, it's as much a ministry as it is a business. One of my favorite quotes is by Theodore Roosevelt: 'People don't care how much you know until they know how much you care.' By doing events I've learned that people desire to be heard and validated. It's not uncommon for ladies to open up and tell me about their life. In the age of electronic devices and hours of screen time, listening is now a lost art. One of my most memorable examples was at our busiest show of the year. There was a little girl around the age of seven with curly brown hair and the bluest eyes we had ever seen. She was blind. My husband had a strong desire to pray for her. He asked her parents for permission, and they excitedly said, "Yes, please do!" Lots of people were in our booth, but it didn't matter. When we finished praying, another lady in my tent began to weep and asked us to pray for her as well. She was only fifty years young and already dealing with Parkinson's disease. All four of us, her husband and mine, grabbed hands and we prayed for this new friend. People like to see the 'real you,' not a salesy you! Although we may have missed sales, we captured their heart and hopefully left a lasting impression, which in turn serves them and us as they become repeat customers and refer their friends.

—Lisa Sutton, Director, Lilla Rose

U is for...

Up

"Fear is the thief of success."
—*Brenda Ster, Sassy Suite*

Up

"Should I sit behind my table and wait for them to ask for help?"
—Marie S., PA

Consistently, at every show, you will see at least some vendors standing up, talking to and interacting with the shoppers. You will see other vendors sitting behind their table reading, on their phone, talking to one another, or knitting. Once or twice I have even seen a vendor sleeping. Also, consistently, the ones who are up and engaging with the crowd yield higher sales and leads. Stand up. You are there to serve and help shoppers. You are there to be available to assist them and help make their coming to that event a pleasant experience. Stand on the side of your table, ready to greet those passing by and engage them in conversation if possible. Do not block their view or ability to approach your display, or someone else's for that matter. If no one is nearby, turn and face the front of your display and merchandise. Merchandising is when you move things around and straighten your display. This not only keeps your display neat and tidy, it also gives the appearance of a customer at your table which will draw others over to see what "the customer" is looking at. This is a natural phenomenon and one of the best crowd magnets you could ever create! If you have helpers with you at your booth, have them join you. The more the merrier! You will soon have shoppers stepping up to get a closer look, at which point you step to the side, welcoming them and offering to help or asking a question to engage them in conversation.

Everything changed the day I stood in front of my booth. Direct sales was as far from my wheelhouse as you could get. Then I found a product that I was passionate about and just knew I had to share it with everyone. But I was green to the world of direct sales. I knew I loved the product, but had no clue on how to approach selling it. My first event was a learning lesson like no other! I was allowed to set up the night before, so I would be all ready to go bright and early the next day. I remember getting home that night and changing my booth a million times in my head as I lay awake full of emotions. *What if I failed? What if people didn't love what I had to share with them as much as I did? What am I doing?*

The next morning came quick. I was up and excited to seize the day! Sell it all! I arrived and quickly realized I had *no idea* what I was supposed to do. I changed my setup three or four times, then started watching the other vendors to see what they were doing. They were all sitting behind their booths, reading books, on their phones, or sleeping! So, I quietly sat behind my booth and read through a product catalog. I did okay that day, for my first time, but I was bored. It took me a few more shows and some research to learn that sitting behind my booth might still get me a few sales, but it was no way to build a business.

When I stood in front of my booth and interacted with customers and vendors, things really started to change for me! My sales went up, I started to build a team, and I developed personally. I discovered things about myself that only experience could give me. It wasn't just about what I was selling, it was the relationships I was building! I believe that day that I stood up was the start of why the team we have built is so wonderful and so strong!

—Wendy Gundlach, Director, Lilla Rose

V is for...
Variety

"Prepare yourself for two kinds of people: those who want to know you, and those who want to know your product."
—*Becky & Kevin Preece, Scentsy Independent Super Star Directors*

Variety

"What should I do if I feel like my customer doesn't 'click' with me?"
—*Jessica B., PA*

You are going to meet a variety of people while working at vendor events. This is a great thing! Awareness of this will help you be prepared to offer fabulous customer service and care to everyone you encounter.

- Be interested in all of them.
- Share a smile and a kind word with everyone.
- Ask them questions and engage them to see what they are interested in. Don't make assumptions about any of them. Do not assume by their age, gender, or appearance that they would or would not be interested in what you have to offer. Instead, make it your goal to get to know them a bit and

see what they like and need and then determine together if you really and sincerely do have a product or service that might match their wants and needs.

Perhaps you really don't have what they want or need but you saw a fellow vendor on another aisle that does. Let them know! They will see that your genuine interest is in helping them and that is a win for you both! You never know when interactions like that will come back to grow your business in the form of them recommending someone else to you!

W is for...
What They Want & Wise Words

"Be a gazelle: swiftly change course when you meet an obstacle. Instead of using emotional energy to complain or rehash drama, use that energy to make a new plan and figure out how to move forward. Successful people take responsibility and they focus on SOLUTIONS, not problems."
—*Charlotte Siems, Plexus, Diamond Ambassador*

What They Want

"How can I determine what my customer really needs or wants so that I can better serve them?" — *Elizabeth R., OH*

In his most popular book, "How to Win Friends and Influence People," Dale Carnegie says, "Ultimately, people will do things for their reasons, not ours." This is so true! At a craft or vendor show, people are not going to shop with you because you need or want them to. You must put yourself in their shoes. You must figure out what they want, and then help them get it. Typically, if a person wants something, or thinks they need something, they will figure this out on their own and go out and get that thing. However, there are many times that a person has not yet realized what they want or need. At a show, you have a fabulous opportunity to show them how what you have meets a need or a want that they have not even realized they have! First, you find out how what you have solves problems for others. Not just what it does or even what you like, but what problems it solves, what solutions it provides.

- Do you sell bags? What problems do they solve? Might the shoppers have a purse with no pockets and they can't find anything, and one of your bags has great compartments to help them easily find their phone, and a hook so they stop losing their keys? Seriously. I need that in my life. I can't tell you how many times I get to my car, with my arms filled with bags or packages, and then can't find or if I find, can't reach, the keys at the bottom of my purse!

- Do you sell hair accessories? What problems do they solve? I cannot wear 99% of the hair accessory products in the drug stores because they are tight and give me horrible headaches. A hair accessory that looks pretty but doesn't give me a headache? I'd be all over that! That's why I fell in love with my company and our products years ago!

- Do you sell warmers and scented wax melts? These are good for people with young children where an open flame candle may not be safe. Another problem you solve is the black soot that develops on the walls from lighting candles and the dangerous possibility of candles being left on or knocked over and starting a fire.

What problems do the items you sell or services you provide solve for shoppers? List here some creative ways you can communicate those solutions to shoppers at your next event.

_____

_____

_____

_____

Your shoppers are on their way to becoming your long-time customers when they walk away feeling good about themselves and that they bought something they wanted and needed rather then a yucky feeling of having been sold to.

Here's a problem I struggle with. I have no idea how to pick out the best color for my face powder. I try to shop in the stores, I've ordered online, and I seriously cannot get the right shade. One day, I met a makeup rep at an event and let her try. Success! She knew her product line, took the time to ask me what help I needed, and then took the time to find the right shade. I can promise you that I would not have gone up to her and asked for help. If she didn't come up to me and specifically say, "What is it that you are needing today and how can I help you find it?" I would have casually browsed and walked away not wanting to waste any more money guessing on the right shade for my skin. When I answered, "Oh, I'm just looking really, I'm not really into nice makeup. I'm not good at picking out the right stuff," she replied, "That's what I'm here for!" And then she went on to describe my skin tone and the colors that would work best for me. She not only offered to help, she asked questions to get me engaged, she focused on solutions, she listened to my answer, and hit a homerun by heading in the exact direction I needed to go with her next comment. She then took the time to patiently help me. I never felt pressured or rushed. She complimented how pretty I looked after she sampled the products. I left feeling great about myself, my look, and her! And I had a nice bag of new makeup that included way more than just the face powder! You can see how her sincere style wound up being a win for her as well!

—Shannon

Wise Words

"What words should I stay away from when speaking to customers?"
—Marie S., PA

Choosing your words wisely is an important component in helping shoppers become comfortable with you and eventually become your customers, hostesses, and team members. Beyond that, your words have power. The power to hurt or the power to really impact someone in a great way. Too often in life our words and our actions scream to the world, "Hey! Look at me! Check me out!" We do this because everyone else is also completely consumed with only themselves and we feel like we aren't getting enough attention or recognition. One approach is what everyone is already doing. Screaming louder, trying to be the one to get the attention on themselves. I suggest a different approach. Come alongside others. Use the power of your words to lift them up. Put *them* in the spotlight. Recognize *their* contributions, tell them what you appreciate about them. Listen to what they have to say. Smile. Pay attention. Then ask them to tell you more. You don't need to scream to be in the spotlight or get attention. Trust me, if you care about people and use your opportunity to listen instead of talk and build *them* up instead of yourself, you *will be* in the spotlight.

- When you speak to your customers, hostesses, and team, ask yourself if your words are:
  o Condemning or supportive
  o Crushing or inspiring
  o Focused on self or focused on serving
  o Downers or uppers
- When speaking about your products or company, be careful not to exclude anyone by using jargon and terms only those "in the know" understand. Avoid words such as:
  o Compensation
  o Uplines, downlines
  o UPP or CP
  o PV, GV, or whatever you use to mention your sales volume.
  o OFS, PSA
  o PEQA, TIA
  o Kitnapping
  o Sub A Sales
- Make the most of every conversation by intentionally thinking about and preparing which words you will use in various situations.

- o When talking to a possible new team member, using the word "agreement" instead of "contract" projects a more joint venture and is less confining.

- o Using the word "investment" instead of "cost" or "price" increases the perceived value of the exchange.

- Using your words to try to pressure someone or manipulate them is not a way to grow a relationship or a business. It's a way to kill one. People respond best, and without later regret, to genuine interest, sincerity, and value.

  - o I once heard a direct sales representative explain to consultants in her company, "It takes money to make money! That's why I only work with winners!" Anyone new, less experienced, or struggling even slightly with self-doubt will shrink back even further into their shell after that comment. Winners can be developed from anyone, anyplace, at any time. How you choose to use your words could be the very inspiration someone needs to make a great decision and great strides towards success.

  - o After the product demonstration, a sales person in our home once ended his presentation with, "I'm pretty busy, so I'm hoping we can wrap this up tonight."
    Talk about pressure! His attempt at sounding "so busy" and "so successful" and hoping to pressure us into signing on the dotted line that night so he could get on with his other customers and we wouldn't miss out on his "fabulous" offer totally backfired. I saw right through his pushy sales tactics and so will your customers if you use the same approach. The ones who cave and buy under pressure are also the ones most likely to regret that purchase, return it, or at the very least not buy from you again or refer people to you because you didn't make them feel comfortable, you made them feel pressured.

  - o Statements like, "Our products always..." or "Our company never..." will not have the effect you might desire. You think you are being convincing. In reality, always and never are never always accurate.

Rather than convince them that what you are saying is true, you are leaving them wondering if they can trust what you say.

Making a firm commitment to use only positive words, or no words when you are listening, is a great way to make impressive first impressions and develop the like, know, and trust factor in everyone you meet. Wrong words send conversations in the wrong direction, send wrong messages, and push people the wrong way during presentations. Make the most of every interaction and every conversation by choosing wise words.

X is for...
eXtra

"Collect less likes; change more hearts. Don't share your products, services, or opportunity for your own ego and vanity. Instead, use the few seconds or minutes you have in someone's life to truly make a difference! When you come from this approach, everything from marketing to recruiting will change."
—*Lindsay Tompkins, Social Media Trainer, Step into Success*

eXtra

"What is something I can do above and beyond to make my business succeed?"
—*Wendy G., WI*

What extra can you do, or what extra value can you provide that will help you stand out from the other vendors? Review all of the *Success Unwrapped* chapters as they each contain ways to help you stand out and maximize every opportunity and potential at your events. Try a few from the list below as well:

- Stop talking and start listening. There is no better way to serve others than to find out what it is they want, need, and desire, and then help them get it! If you do all the talking, expect them to listen, and hope they will be interested in what you sell, you've missed the point of serving. Instead of doing all the talking, ask more questions and listen to their answers. Consider basic questions that you can ask anyone and come up with some specific questions that might help you determine if they might want, desire, or need something you have to offer. Some examples to get you started include:

- Are you shopping for anything special today?

- Do you have any gift needs you are hoping to find?

Depending on what you sell, you might ask questions about their style and preferences in certain areas.

- With every decision you make, think of your customers first. What will make it easiest for them? What will make the experience of shopping with you more pleasurable? A great example of this is accepting credit cards. We know they have limited cash and will likely need it for lunch or other vendors that can't accept credit cards. Make it easy for them. Be the one who is happy to take their card, isn't worried about the little percentage that goes to the card reader company, and is pleased you were able to make it easier on them.

- Extra extras. When you are out shopping or at a festival or some type of event, if someone has a bowl of candy on their table, do you enjoy that? Do you take one? Are you grateful for that little treat? While you are taking one, do you give them just a minute, at least, of your time to see what they are selling? Yeah, me too. It doesn't take much to put a little candy in a bowl. Yet it can yield happy shoppers who will now give you and your booth the time of day. If you know there will be a lot of children at an event, and the moms will want to shop, consider a little bowl of stickers for the children. If you have the space, add a little table with simple coloring pages for the children while Mom browses your selection. My daughter was able to set up a little table and offered face painting for the children at a few of my shows. It was a big hit and a great crowd magnet.

- Packaging and gift wrap. Especially during busy holiday seasons, shoppers appreciate the added touch of their gifts being wrapped or packaged in a special way.

- Show them and tell them you appreciate them. Before you hand them their bag, look at their contact information they completed on the order form. Take a quick glance at their name and use it when you thank them. "Susan, it was great to meet you today! Thank you so much for your purchase. If I can be of any help to you, my contact information is in right in your bag. I'll touch base with you soon to be sure you are happy with everything." Then, make sure that you do!

- Be reliable. Be someone they can trust to do what you said you were going to do. If you tell a shopper you will reach out to ensure they are satisfied, then do that. You will not be bugging them, you will be honoring your word and caring enough to be sure they are happy customers and know you are available to help them should they need it.

- Be sincere. Really and truly get yourself to the point where you do not care if they don't buy from you. That should not be your goal. Helping them, making their day, or putting a smile on a face are your goals. Two things will then happen. First, you will always have a successful day, and second, you will wind up with a lot of sales and business growth! The sales are not the goal, rather, the result of your sincere, reliable, appreciative, "other's first" style. People will be drawn to you and want to shop with you, host for you, and join your team.

- Leave them feeling good! Have you ever known a person that whenever you are around them you just feel good? There is something about them. Maybe you just can't put your finger on it, but you leave feeling good, better about yourself, better about your day, better about what is to come. That type of person has a gift. A gift of caring more about others and putting others in the spotlight instead of themselves. It blows our mind as we walk away that they cared about us, asked about us, and seemed genuinely interested in our answers. Here's the coolest thing, they aren't just like that with you! They are like that with almost everyone, and you can tell because everyone wants to be their friend and be around them. It's not a gift you have to be born with! You can learn how to be like that too! It takes focus and practice. At first, you might not really consider yourself a "people person." In fact, you might not like small talk or meeting new people. But given time and concentrated effort in asking questions, keeping the focus on them, and what is going on in their life, listening when they talk, and not just waiting for your turn to tell your story, you will start to realize what an absolute privilege and joy it is to get to meet and know interesting new people. People are fascinating! When you are in sales, remember, you are in the business of building relationships with people. Go that eXtra mile so people leave their time with you feeling great about themselves!

Y is for...
You

"It is easy to lose yourself when you are thinking
of others. While selflessness is one of the greatest of
qualities, it is not selfish to take time for you."
—*Becky & Kevin Preece, Scentsy Independent Super Star Directors*

You

"How do you make time to eat when you get busy?" *—Mona J, PA*

I have found that shoppers and even family and friends sometimes think that working at a craft show or vendor event is not actually "work." Some have the impression that direct sales and selling at an event is not a serious business venture. Others assume it's just playtime or too easy to be considered work. Still others think it's a total waste of your time. They don't understand and have not experienced this industry personally.

Try not to take it personally. I would encourage you to embrace the exciting fact that you *are* a business owner! When you fully unwrap all the possibilities and apply my secrets to a successful show, your business is going to soar! You can then laugh their comments away while earning a six-figure income for doing something "so cute" that they think isn't really "work work."

After working hundreds of events myself, I can assure you that when you put in your full effort and apply the secrets we unwrapped in this book, what you will be doing very much qualifies as work. Rewarding work, but still work! If you are just starting in the show circuit, plan on getting used to lugging heavy tables, tents, and boxes around. Plan on exerting a lot of mental energy in your preparations and display. Be prepared for long days that can be hard on your feet, legs, and back. Remaining positive and outgoing, even when circumstances are not optional, can be emotionally exhausting!

You need to take care of yourself. Plan ahead and be prepared so you don't get sick, hurt, or burned out from long, hard, sometimes painfully slow and emotionally draining days working events.

- Get to bed a bit earlier the night before a show. Plenty of rest will go a long way on a busy day.

- Bring and drink plenty of water. I'm a big fan of my coffee, so have some of that too if you are like me. But caffeine dehydrates you. The extra trips to the bathroom, created by drinking enough water, will be worth avoiding the dehydrated headache or day after aches and pains in your muscles from not having enough fluids while putting stress on your body standing most of the day.

- Take bathroom breaks. Even if you are by yourself. Grab your money and your phone and ask a friendly neighbor if they would please keep an eye on your booth for just a few minutes. I have never had someone say no. Your bladder will thank me.

- Bring healthy snacks that are easy to eat between shoppers. This is especially helpful if you are working an event by yourself and can't take a lunch break. A few great options I have found include:
  o Granola and soft granola bars
  o Almonds

- o Bite-sized cheese
- o Dried fruit

Don't pack anything or buy anything for lunch that has a strong or offensive odor or will give you bad breath.

- Bring a treat for you that will make you smile. A bit of chocolate or something else bite size that you enjoy and will give you a little pick me up when the day gets long.

- Wear comfortable shoes.

- Invest in an anti-fatigue mat for the floor. Even a small one will be worth the investment. It won't cover the entire floor, but when you are walking around, you won't feel as much stress on your body. When the crowd is slow, and you are in one place for longer, strategically place the mat where you will be standing.

- Be prepared for temperature changes to stay comfortable. Dress in layers so you can stay cool or warm as needed. It's hard to serve shoppers well when your hands are freezing or you're so hot you feel like you could pass out!

- Prepare for your events ahead of time so you are not rushed. Pack and load up your car the day before. Trust me on this one. I can't tell you how many times I've just not felt like it the night before and then woke up to see it's raining or snowing. In those times, I say to myself, "You should have just done it last night!"

- If possible, give yourself the day after the event off. Adrenaline, especially at a busy, exciting show, can keep you going and you might not realize the toll the long day is taking. It may not be until you have sat down, driven home, and then gotten out of the car that your body says, "Hey! No more of that standing and walking stuff! All done for the day, thanks!"

Z is for...
Zigzag

"Turbulence is the price you pay for flying high. Don't give up."
—Rachel Ortense, 2 Star Crown Purium Health Products

Zigzag

"What happens when life takes over and you lose focus of your goals?"
—Jessica B., PA

Things don't always go as planned. Not in life, and not in business. Unexpected twists and turns are zigzags we all will be confronted with.

Anyone can book and "do" a craft show. But not everyone will yield successful results. Vendor events, like any area of your business, require investment. Investment in the form of money, sometimes a lot of time in long or even multiple days, and for many, the possibility of physical and emotional exertion. One of the saddest things I see in the direct sales industry is consultants investing their time, money, and effort and leaving an event feeling they lost in all departments. As a top leader and seller in this industry, I've fallen in love with craft and vendor events and learned, sometimes the hard way, what works and what does not. I've unwrapped all my best secrets and successful practices so you can walk away from every single craft show knowing in one way or another, it was a success!

Even when we feel at the top of our game and are finally moving in the right direction, zigzags happen.

As the famous Zig Ziglar once said, "Your response-or reaction-to the negative reveals what's inside of you. It exposes your heart and shows the kind of person you really are."

You know what? *You* are a great person! That's who you really are!

When zigzags throw you off balance, it's time to remember your "why," try again, start fresh, and recommit to never quitting. You can do this!

I don't want to leave you with the impression that everything is going to be perfect and amazing if you follow my advice, A–Z. Everyone faces obstacles and has struggles, even at a seemingly perfect event following the best practices. What you do when those obstacles come, how you respond, can make all the difference. I suggest you wad them up, toss them under the table, and move on! Let me explain.

At my biggest show of the entire year, where over 30,000 guests attend, I was working alone. The crowds were plentiful, and my sales were soaring. There was only one thing wrong. I was following my own advice and staying hydrated and the natural consequence of drinking water was upon me. I had to go! I grabbed my money pouch, let my vendor neighbor know I would be back as fast as possible, and zoomed to the ladies' room. I think I broke a record for the fastest time in and out and literally ran down the aisle back to my booth. I just knew that I'd arrive and find a swarm of ladies checking out my products and waiting to be helped. I was right! A crowd had formed in my absence. I didn't waste a moment! I jumped right in, offering to help size the ladies with the hair accessories on display. One, then another, then another. I was feeling amazing! On top of my game! Adrenaline had taken over! I zipped around to face the even larger crowd and let them know I'd be happy to size them all. At that moment, a woman from the crowd leaned forward and quietly said, "I just had to tell you…" In my head, in one of those split seconds where you have a complete thought without really enough time to have it, I thought to myself, "Man, she is going to say, 'These are amazing!' or 'Phew! You are incredible! You just jumped right in there and helped us all so fast!' Not even close. She leaned closer and said, "You have a long piece of toilet paper hanging out of the back of your pants."

I had just run through the aisle, past twenty tables and hundreds of shoppers, and stood with my back to my own crowd sizing ladies with hair clips, all the while trailing a tail of TP!

What could I do? Certainly, this was one of the most embarrassing moments of my career.

Without hesitation, I thanked her, grabbed that TP, wadded it up in a ball, tossed it under my table, out of sight, and immediately said, "Who's next and ready to be sized?"

Don't let any obstacles or struggles hold you back from unwrapping your success!

Wad and toss! Wad and toss! Keep on plowing ahead! That show and that day wound up being my most successful day in my craft show history!

Wad-toss-move on!

Whatever company you are with, whatever products or service you sell, however you work your business, the gift of success is yours to unwrap! Never give in, never give up, and never say, it's the end.

—Shannon

Resources

Book Bonus:

Link to the Open Date Card and Show Tracker Form:
  www.bit.ly/SuccessUnwrappedBookBonus

Contact Shannon:

www.ShannonFerraby.com
Shannon@ShannonFerraby.com
www.lillarose.biz/greateights

Endorsements:

Bob Burg: coauthor of The Go-Giver and The Go-Giver Influencer,
  www.burg.com

John Dorsey: CEO, Lilla Rose, Inc.

Melanie Moore: CinchShare Director of Training and Development,
  melanie@cinchshare.com, www.cinchshare.com

Chapter Quote Contributing Leaders and Trainers:

Becky Preece: Scentsy Super Star Director & Founding Consultant,
  www.whatascent.scentsy.us

Brenda Ster: Sassy Suite, www.sassysuite.com

Carla New: Origami Owl Senior Director carlanew.origamiowl.com

Carly Reeves: Black Status Level 2 Presenter, Younique, www.lashballer.com

Charlot Nagai: Executive Director, Pampered Chef, www.CharlottsWeb.com

Charlotte Siems: Diamond Ambassador, Plexus, www.charlottesiems.com

Conni Brown: Premier Team Leader, Perfectly Posh, www.conni.po.sh

Emily Chandler: Founding Star Director, Keep Collective, www.liveacharminglife.com

Emily Roberts: Plexus Diamond Ambassador, www.StraightFromTheER.com

Jessica Fogarty: Unit Organizer, Princess House, www.JessicaFogarty.com

Kalen Clark: Group Director, Steeped Tea, www.KalenClark.com

Lindsay Tompkins: Social Media Trainer, www.stepintosuccess.com

Melissa Dettmer: Independent Sales Consultant, Vice President Sales Leader, Norwex, www.melissadettmer.norwex.biz

Melissa Fietsam: Directly Social with Melissa Fietsam, www.directlysocial.com

Michelle Withers: Creative Success Systems, www.creativesuccesssystems.com

Nancy Ann Wartman: Director, Usborne Books & More, www.facebook.com/UsborneUSA

Paula Ramm: Lilla Rose, Jr. Executive, www.CoastalConservatory.com

Rachel Ortense: 2 Star Crown, Purium Health Products, www.Rachelortense.com

Shelli Auger: Brand Partner & Trainer, Yelloow, www.shelliauger.com

Tamara Allen: Founding Director Magnolia and Vine, tamaraallen88@gmail.com